W9-BMS-846

REMEMBER MY *Soul*

LORI PALATNIK with RABBI YAAKOV PALATNIK

WHAT TO DO IN MEMORY
OF A LOVED ONE

A Path of Reflection and Inspiration for
Shiva, the Stages of Jewish Mourning, and Beyond

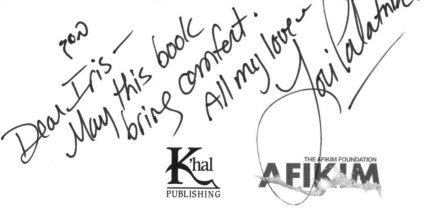

בס"ד

Dear Iris —
May this book
bring comfort.
All my love ~
Lori Palatnik

Khal
PUBLISHING

THE AFIKIM FOUNDATION
AFIKIM

Copyright © 1998, 2006 Lori Palatnik with Rabbi Yaakov Palatnik
Second Printing July 2013

ALL RIGHTS RESERVED

No part of this book may be reproduced in any form, photocopy, electronic media, or otherwise, without written permission from the copyright holder, except by a reviewer who wishes to quote brief passages with a review written for inclusion in magazines or newspapers.

THE RIGHTS OF THE COPYRIGHT HOLDER WILL BE STRONGLY ENFORCED.

Published by **K'hal Publishing**
in conjunction with **The Afikim Foundation**
111 John Street, Suite 1720
New York, NY 10038
212-791-7450
www.afikimfoundation.org

Layout & Design	Rachel Block, Block Design/blockdesign@gmail.com
Copyedit	PeopleSpeak

Distributed by MESORAH PUBLICATIONS, LTD.,
    4401 Second Avenue, Brooklyn, NY, 11232 / www.artscroll.com

Distributed in Israel by SIFRIATI/A. GITLER, 6 Hayarkon Street / Bnei Brak 51127

Distributed in Europe by LEHMANNS, Unit E, Viking Business Park,
    Rolling Mill Road / Jarrow, Tyne and Wear, NE32 3DP/ England

Distributed in Australia and New Zealand by GOLDS WORLD OF JUDAICA,
    3-13 William Street / Balaclava, Melbourne 3183 / Victoria Australia

Distributed in South Africa by KOLLEL BOOKSHOP,
    Ivy Common / 105 William Road / Norwood 2192, Johannesburg, South Africa

ISBN: 978-1-60204-014-4

Printed in the United States of America.

Dedicated in Loving Memory of

Harry and Anne Lerner

and

David and Lillian Bober

Whose example of love, commitment, and affection
continue as a living legacy to us all.

From their loving grandchildren and great-grandchildren.

In special memory of Sharona Ellen Lerner.

Dedicated in Loving Memory of

Mrs. Anne "Buby" Nashman

by

The Nashman Family

May her memory be a blessing.

Dedicated by the Author in Loving Memory of

Mrs. Judith Dan

"She was robed in strength and dignity, and she smiled at the future . . ."

Dedicated in Loving Memory of

Yeshiah ben Chaim

Your love of life and your love for us live on.
May the merit of this book be an *aliyah* (elevation)
of your *neshama* (soul). We miss you.

Yaakov and Lori

Shoshana, Zev, Moshe, Bracha Leah, Malkie and Adam

Table of Contents

Acknowledgments

M y husband Yaakov, my greatest fan and my keenest critic. Though I did the actual writing of this book, my husband's scholarship, expertise, and guidance is present on every page. As a rabbi and friend, Yaakov has guided numerous individuals and families through the difficulties of dealing with a loss. This book is truly our book.

With tremendous gratitude, I also want to thank the following people who were instrumental in making this book a reality:

- Gail Prince, for asking.
- Shimon Apisdorf of Leviathan Press, for believing.
- Rabbi Noah Weinberg, Rosh HaYeshiva of Aish HaTorah, my rabbi and teacher, for all the Torah. Every word in this book is inspired by you. Forgive me if in any way I did a disservice to all that you taught me.
- Those who recently experienced a loss and kindly read the manuscript and offered support and suggestions. I am honored if the book gave you some measure of comfort at such a difficult time.
- My neighbor, Bobby, who made me realize I was on to something when he faithfully read an early manuscript while mourning his father. He told me the only thing bad about the manuscript was that it left him "wanting to learn more."
- Rabbi Mitch Mandel of Aish HaTorah Toronto, who shared some beautiful words of Torah with me that he shares with those who he comforts through loss.
- Those who shared memories of losing a loved one with me. Fresh tears were shed as they relived very painful times so that others could gain comfort.
- My children, who supported me through the many hours of "writing Ima's new book."

- Special thanks to Elana Schwartz, mother's helper extraordinaire, who made sure I spent that summer writing while my children were well cared for.
- My sponsors, who made it possible. May this book be a merit to you and your loved ones.
- The Almighty, for blessing me in every way.

Note to the reader: Generally, references to *halacha* (Jewish law), have been reviewed by Rabbinic authorities. Any inadvertent errors are the sole mistake of the author and are no reflection on the rabbis and scholars who generously gave of their time to read and give guidance to the book *Remember My Soul*.

Introduction:

A Late Night Call
From a Neighbor

We had just moved into the neighborhood. Boxes upon boxes still lay open, some unpacked, others barely touched. As I sat in the cluttered living room, the phone rang. It was my new neighbor across the street. We exchanged pleasantries. She welcomed me to the neighborhood and talked about shopping and schools. Then she paused. The silence was not awkward but thoughtful. She obviously had more on her mind.

"Um, I know your husband is a rabbi, and I had a kind of funny conversation with my daughter last night at bedtime."

"Did you want to speak to my husband?" I offered.

"No," she answered, "It wasn't a serious thing. You see, I was tucking my daughter Amanda in. She's eight, and she turned and asked me, 'Mommy, what happens to people after they die?' And I felt bad because I had to tell her that according to Judaism, nothing happens after you die."

Nothing happens after you die? I was speechless. I was shocked. Swallowing hard and choosing my words carefully, I said, "But that's not what we believe at all."

"It's not?" she answered, surprised and relieved.

"No, it's not."

"Then what do we believe?"

I pulled up a chair and sat down. This was going to be a long conversation. I started from the beginning and walked her through the subject. We were on the phone the entire evening, explaining, discussing, and questioning.

Since that night, I have come to realize that Jews have many misconceptions about their own religion, but this is probably the most common: that Judaism has no belief in the afterlife. The ideas set forth in the first section of this book are ideas from our tradition that my husband and I have had cause to share time and time again. They are not depressing or morbid, but rather enlightening and uplifting. These concepts do not change a person's death, but they certainly can change a person's life. I think you will see what we mean.

Section One:

What Happens
After You Die?

*A*re you a body or a body and a soul? Most people would answer, "I'm a body and a soul." But do we mean it? Do we live our lives and make decisions as if each of us is not just a body but a body and a soul?

At certain times in our lives, we reconnect with our souls. A wedding is a soul experience for the bride and groom, a new beginning through the spiritual union under the *chuppah* (the wedding canopy).

For many, going to Israel is a life-altering experience of connecting with the land, the people, and the legacy that are part of every Jew.

The birth of a child is a soul-stirring moment. We witness the miracle of creation, the wonder of a new life, and we feel the awesome responsibility of this priceless gift to guide through life.

On a journey to the countryside, as we look up to a star-filled sky, we can truly see forever. A feeling of transcendence overtakes us.

A near-death experience can be a dramatic soul encounter. People do not recover from such experiences without realizing that they have been given another chance. Afterward, each new day holds new meaning, and even casual relationships turn precious.

Death itself puts us in touch with our souls. No one stands at a funeral and thinks about the menu for dinner that night. Everyone thinks, "What is life all about, anyway?" "What am I living for?" "Is there something beyond this world?"

We know that we are souls. When we look into the eyes of someone we love, we do not see random molecules thrown together. We love the essence of that person, and that essence is what we call a *neshama*, a "soul."

> God formed man out of dust of the ground, and breathed into his nostrils a breath (soul) of life. (Genesis 2:7)

The soul is eternal, although the body's existence is temporary.[1] When God decides that a person's time on this earth has ended, He takes back the soul, and the body returns to the earth, completing the cycle of creation ("dust to dust"). For in the beginning, the first person, Adam, was created from the dust of the ground.

The essence of our departed loved ones, the goodness and special qualities that they possessed, the part of them that made noble choices in life, performed good deeds, and touched the lives of others—their *neshama*—goes on to a world of infinite pleasure. In that world, physical sufferings do not exist, and souls bask in the light of their Creator, enjoying the rewards for all that they did here on earth.[2]

But what kinds of choices and deeds count? Those of people who saved the lives of others, who led armies to victory, who discovered medical cures? Yes, those people enjoy a place in the World to Come, but so do those who led simpler lives, who performed quiet acts of kindness and made a difference to those around them. Perhaps what they did wasn't front-page news, but small acts have merit too and can mean an eternity of the deepest pleasures in the World to Come.

What we are experiencing now is called Olam Hazeh (this world), while the next world is referred to as Olam Habah (the World to Come). We are all familiar with what happens here, but what goes on in Olam Habah?

Of course no one in Jewish history ever died and came back to tell us what happens in the world beyond.[3] Yet we are assured that there is another existence. Maimonides, the twelfth-century scholar, included this belief in his "Thirteen Principles of Faith." Our oral tradition speaks about it at length, and Kabbalah, Jewish mysticism, is also replete with wisdom about the hereafter.[4]

Olam Habah (the World to Come) is more easily understood when compared to a theater. Our sages state that every Jew has a portion in the World to Come.[5] This means that a seat in the theater has been reserved for each person's soul. But as in any theater, some seats are better than others.

If God is "center stage," some souls will enjoy seats in the front row, center section, others will sit in the balcony, and some will have obstructed views, but everyone will have a place. The seats we are assigned are based on the choices we make and the deeds that we do in Olam Hazeh, this world.[6]

We are told that we will be surprised who gets the best seats.[7] We will look down and say, "What are they doing there? They weren't so great!" "What are they doing up front? They didn't accomplish very much!" And God will answer and say, "They are there because they listened to My voice."

We make a mistake when we think that only those who seem great, honored, and accomplished will merit a place before God. Each person is judged individually, and we don't know what difference one *mitzvah*, one act of kindness, will make when God reviews a person's life.[8] Listening to God does not only mean obeying the laws of what to do and what not to do. Hearing His voice means that we see life isn't ruled by coincidence, that we realize events take place for a reason, and that we act accordingly. We may not know the Torah backward and forward, but if we have a relationship with our Creator, that can be worth a front-row seat in eternity.

Our sages say that if we took all of our life's pleasures, every one of them, and all the pleasures of everyone in this world and brought them all together, the total wouldn't be worth even one second in the World to Come,[9] the pleasure of being close to God.[10]

Now, this pleasure may not have been uppermost in our minds in this world, but we know that if we were called to someone's home for a meeting, and following the meeting the host announced that God's presence was about to arrive and wanted to communicate with us, we wouldn't say, "Well, sorry, it's getting late and I have to get up early tomorrow." We would be scared out of our minds; but nothing is more important or more desirable than going before God, Creator of heaven and earth.

We can't imagine passive pleasure. For us pleasure is active. We go away on vacation. We ask for a raise and get it. We eat a big helping of the flavor of the month. Something happens and we feel pleasure. So how can sitting in one place be so overwhelmingly pleasurable? Because it is an earned plea-sure—what we did in our lifetime on earth has yielded this result.

In Olam Habah we are sitting before God, who created us. He knows us inside and out. Every moment here on earth is His gift to us. He loves us more than our parents love us, more than we love our children.[11] And He has called us back to Him.

Of course people are not perfect and we all make mistakes, but those errors in judgment do not erase our good deeds. If we light candles on Friday night and then go to a movie, God does not look down and say, "Candles. Movie. We're back to square one." The act of lighting candles, the bringing in of Shabbat, is eternal. Nothing can take it away. It is the same with every positive effort we make in life.[12]

We all make bad decisions sometimes, and some acts we deeply regret. What should we do about them? Ideally, we should take care of our mistakes here in this life. If we have wronged someone, we should make peace. If we are letting bad habits or character hold us back, we should work on breaking free and return to being the person we know we can be.

When our souls leave this world and go before God, we give an accounting, and a certain judgment takes place.[13] Judgment is not something we look forward to. Who wants to be judged? But this is not just any judge. This is God, our Father in Heaven. A human judge might be biased. But this is our Creator, who gave us life and everything that happens in our lives. His judgment of us comes from love, and anything that derives from love is for our good.[14]

Further, His judgment means that our judgments count. Life is not random; it has meaning and purpose. The decisions that we make in our lives count for something, and not just at the moment but forever. The ulti-mate reward and punishment happen, but only in Olam Habah, the next world, not here in Olam Hazeh, this world.[15]

But what about that bonus at work? I know that God was rewarding me for giving charity. And that time my car broke down? That was a punishment for not driving my mother to her hair appointment.

This idea is a little bit right and a little bit wrong. It's right to realize that events happen in life for a reason and that they are from God. But it's wrong to think that God is rewarding us for our good deeds or punishing us for our errors.[16] What is really going on is that God is communicating with us.[17] When we give charity or do anything that is right and good, God doesn't reward us, but He does give us more opportunities to do good.

The car breaking down is not a punishment but a message. Only you know what God is telling you.[18] Receive the message and learn from it.[19]

Each year on Rosh Hashanah and Yom Kippur, God judges us. He looks at the deeds and choices that we made during the year and decides what our next year will be like based on our efforts to correct our mistakes and the decisions that we made in our lives.[20] But at the time of death, after the burial, we go before God who will judge us not just on one year but on our entire lives.[21]

The soul will go to one of two places: Heaven, which we have discussed, or Gehenom, Hell.

We believe in Hell? It may be surprising, perhaps, but yes, we do.[22] Why is it a surprise? Often it is a subject not brought up in Hebrew school or in the synagogues. But also the reality is that we grow up in a Christian world, where as youngsters we understand that anything Christian is not ours. And therefore, if Christians believe in Heaven and Hell, then we don't.

But we do. Yet the Jewish understanding of Heaven and Hell differs from what we may hear from other religions.

Hell is a place God created to help us take care of the mistakes we didn't correct in this world. It is called Gehenom. But don't be afraid. It's not a place of devils and pitchforks, and it's not forever. If it is God's judgment that a person has to enter Gehenom, the maximum amount of time spent there would be one Jewish year.[23] A person can be there a split second, an entire Jewish year, or somewhere in between. That is the reason that we say Kaddish (the mourner's prayer) for eleven months. We assume that our loved ones would never be there an entire year.[24] Ideally, we want to bypass it all together.

A great rabbi was scheduled to speak on the subject of the next world at an Executive Lunch and Learn series in downtown Toronto. My husband picked him up at the airport and on the way downtown asked him to "go easy on Gehenom" with the primarily non-religious audience. He was afraid the rabbi would scare them.

The rabbi turned to my husband and asked, "Do you have hospitals here in Toronto?"

"Yes," he answered, confused.

"And," continued the rabbi, "are these world-class hospitals?"

"Yes," answered my husband again.

"Would you ever want to check in to these hospitals?"

"No," said my husband.

"But if you need to, aren't you glad they're there?"

The rabbi explained that Gehenom is a hospital for the soul. Going there will be painful. But it's because of God's kindness, His mercy, and His love that such a place exists. We wouldn't want to check in even for a minute, but if we have to, we know it's for our good, and we hope our stay will be as short as possible.

The way to avoid Gehenom altogether is to take care of our mistakes here. This is not an easy task, but by making the supreme effort in this world, we will ultimately avoid a much greater pain in the next.[25] (See the study of *teshuvah* on Day Twenty in Section 2.)

Whether we are able to bypass it or we have to spend some time in Gehenom, eventually we are able to enter the theater of Olam Habah.[26] If we arrive and each of us is assigned a seat, does that mean we are there for eternity and that our share of pleasure is limited to our particular view? No. The people we have left on earth can increase our share in the World to Come and enable us to earn better seating.[27]

How does this happen? In memory of loved ones, people often give charity, name babies, learn Torah, and so on. These are not just good deeds. These are acts we do in this world that have everlasting spiritual ramifications.

When we do something in someone's memory, we are saying, "Because of this person that I loved, I am living my life differently. He may be gone, but he is not forgotten. He continues to be a source of inspiration in my life. His life mattered, and his legacy will continue to make a difference."

What should you do in memory of a loved one?

My husband tells people to take a thirty-day period, ideally the first thirty days after the funeral, which is called the *shloshim* (see "Stage Two: Shloshim" in Section 3.), and do something concrete in memory of the departed. For some it could be placing a coin in a *tzedakah* (charity) box each day and reciting a simple prayer.

Most people, after experiencing such a tremendous loss, feel a great need to do something to honor the departed. Because of the concept of Olam Habah, doing something will not only bring you comfort but also add to the merit of the one that you have lost.

Souls in the next world have an awareness of what goes on here.[28] They don't notice whether it's a cold, cloudy day in your city, but they are aware of when mitzvahs happen here. The souls of our loved ones come to the *chuppahs* and the *bar mitzvahs*. They are there when a grandchild receives the first *siddur* (prayer book). They are there when Friday night candles are lit, when tzedakah (charity) is given in their names, when a baby is born and named after them. By living your life differently because they lived, and because they died, you are choosing to honor them and you are making an impact far greater than you will ever know.

This is because another step exists beyond heaven. Approximately one thousand years after the coming of *Mashiach* (the Messiah) comes something called Techias Hamaysim, the resurrection of the dead. At that time, the bodies and souls of many will come back together, and the world will become a very different world than the one we know now.

But let's back up and walk through the Jewish view of Mashiach. Mashiach means "the anointed one," and we believe he can come under two conditions. One is that the Jewish people are so unified and are on such a high level of spirituality that they are a true "light unto the nations," raising all the world to the ultimate level of value and goodness.[29] Then Mashiach comes as a natural result of the high state of mankind.

The other condition is that the Jewish people are so divided and have fallen to such a low level of spirituality and are such a dim light unto the nations that the whole world falls morally. At the point when so much strife has arisen that we would literally blow ourselves up and destroy the world, then Mashiach has to come in order to save the world.

If he comes under the latter condition (and let's face it, the world seems to be going rapidly in that direction), then a war of all wars will take place. Many will die in this war, Jews and non-Jews, but ultimately it will end, and all the Jews, led by Mashiach, will return to Israel. The Third Temple will be rebuilt, and God's presence will again be connected to this world.

The physical world will remain as we know it. People will still get on planes, buy apartments, and have jobs, but the knowledge of the world will be transformed. It will be a world of incredible clarity. Jews and all nations will know what their responsibilities are and will fulfill them. Peace, harmony, and unity will reign.

Mashiach is a mortal being of flesh and blood. He will live and he will die. Opinions differ in the Talmud, but approximately one thousand years after he comes, the world will be transformed. At that point, all souls here and beyond will face another judgment called Yom HaDin HaGadol—the great judgment day. At that point it will be decided who receives eternity and who does not. Those who merit it will be blessed to have their bodies back, and the world will become Gan Eden, the Garden of Eden. We will finally be back where we started, and this time we won't mess it up.

Those who do not merit eternity will cease to exist in any form, physical or spiritual.

What can wipe out a person's eternity? You can do a lot of mitzvahs and good deeds, but God still has His "red lines." Maimonides lists some of the qualities that can wipe out your eternity. For example, a *ba'al gaavah*, a master of arrogance, has no place in the World to Come. Arrogant people are so filled with themselves, there is no room for others. They certainly have no room for God because they think they are god.

Also, a *ba'al lashon hara*, a master of gossip and slander, has no eternity. The Almighty runs the world *mida keneged mida*, measure for measure. Those who spend their time in gossip and rumor cause people to separate from one another. For them, the measure for measure is that at the end, they are separated from everyone for eternity.

If we do merit the return of our bodies, what do we look like? If we died old, do we look old? If we died with one leg, do we still have one leg?

In eternity, your body will be a reflection of your soul's accomplishments in this world. If you achieved wonderful things spiritually here and led a life of goodness and value, then your body in eternity will reflect that. On the other hand, if you spent your time here focused on your body and not your soul, then in eternity your body will also reflect that.

How much time, resources, and energy do we spend on our bodies here compared with the amount we spend on our souls? The answer should wake all of us up to focus on what is really important. By doing so, you are choosing eternity.

Although the world is not looking so good, and we seem to be headed in the wrong direction, do not despair. September 11 taught us many lessons, including that the whole world can change in a second. That day, the world shifted toward evil and destruction. But we should realize that in one second we can shift it the other way.

You don't know what one deed, one act of kindness, one move toward value and goodness can do. In God's eyes, it can be the one deed that shifts the world in the right direction and toward the best outcome.

Now you have a chance to spend a few minutes each day for thirty days and make a real difference, to the soul of your loved one and to yourself. And who knows, perhaps to all mankind.

Section Two:

What to Do in Memory of a Loved One:

A Thirty-Day Path of Reflection,

Inspiration, and Personal Growth

"After my father died, I felt a tremendous need to do something; something of meaning and significance. I knew I wouldn't say Kaddish *more than once or twice. There had to be something else that I could do to help fulfill that need, and to make a difference."*

Michael, thirty-nine years old, businessman

This section is for Michael and for the thousands of others out there who feel just like him.

he next section of this book is a thirty-day path of learning. Whether your loss was recent or many years ago, you will spend approximately five to ten minutes a day dedicated to the memory of your loved one, learning something from our Jewish heritage. Many of the main ideas central to Judaism will be brought to life. Some will be familiar; others will be new.

Each day begins with the same prayer:

May God remember my [relationship: mother, father, friend, etc.], [his/her name], *in whose merit I am now studying about my heritage of Judaism and the Torah.*

For example, if someone lost a father whose English name was John Stein, whose Jewish name was Moshe, and his father's Jewish name was Avrom, the prayer would go like this:

May God remember my father, Moshe ben Avrom, in whose merit I am now studying about my heritage of Judaism and the Torah.

Or

May God remember my father, John Stein, in whose merit I am now studying about my heritage of Judaism and the Torah.

You may use the English name, but the Hebrew or Jewish name is preferable. For example, you may say, "my mother, Robin Cohen," or "my mother, Rachel bat Yosef Chaim." (*Bat* means "daughter of;" *ben* means "son of.") It's your choice. You can insert both English and Hebrew names if you wish—whatever you feel most comfortable with.

After the five to ten minutes of study, you will end with the following prayer:

> *Our Merciful God in Heaven—May this portion of Torah learning be a merit and a blessing for my* [relationship], [name]. *May* [his/her] *soul be bound in the bond of life. May* [his/her] *resting place be that of peace.*

Space is included for your own thoughts and feelings linked to the theme of learning for each day. Later in the book, people who have experienced a loss share their reflections.

Remember—everything you do here in the memory of those who have departed makes a real difference. You are increasing their share in the World to Come. You are increasing their eternal pleasure.[1]

May God comfort you in your time of sorrow, and may each moment that you are learning be a merit to the one who inspired it, the one you have lost.

Judging Others

May God remember my [relationship], [name], *in whose merit I am now studying about my heritage of Judaism and the Torah.*

Our sages ask, "When are you allowed to judge another person?"[2] The answer: "Never." The explanation given is as follows: Who says your blood is redder than his?[3] In other words, we do not know who is more beloved in the eyes of God.[4] We don't know who is really the better person, the homeless person or the cancer scientist. We don't know what challenges God may have given someone growing up. We meet people in the middle of their life stories, in "chapter 3." We have no idea what went on in chapter 1 and chapter 2, and we certainly don't know what lies ahead in chapters 4, 5, and 6. Yet we are so quick to judge. A person who seems at a low point may in fact have worked very hard and overcome hardship to reach even this level. Others, although they may look righteous and accomplished, may be using only a tiny portion of their talents and skills.

How often have people praised you for something that comes naturally and takes little effort on your part? Perhaps it's an artistic ability or language fluency. Yet other areas of your life that may not come so naturally take a much greater amount of pain and effort. They may not be the areas that shine and attract attention, but you know, and God knows, that they are much more important in terms of self-actualization.

Our tradition says that we can't judge someone unless we've arrived in his or her place.[5] And since we can never be in exactly the same place and life circumstance as another person, we are never allowed to judge anyone.[6]

But this doesn't mean we should be so open-minded that we accept anyone or anything. We can't judge a person, but we can judge actions. Yet even when people make mistakes, we can still see the best in them, love them, and care for them in spite of their mistakes.[7] We see this with our children. Who knows their flaws better than we do? Yet we choose to love them.

Only God can truly judge a person, and His judgment is unique to the individual, not based on a formula. Maimonides said that a person may achieve one merit that could outweigh a lifetime of mistakes.[8]

And what is the first attribute a person is judged on? It is the learning of life wisdom.[9] But that does not mean that the first step in judgment is based on how much we know. It is based on our learning, on how hard we tried to find out what was right. God doesn't expect perfection, but He does expect us to try, in every aspect of our lives.

Our sages teach, "Do not regard yourself as a wicked person."[10] This means it is a mistake even to judge ourselves. We all err in judgment, but each one of us is created in God's image, and to label ourselves stupid, bad, or worthless, is counter to everything in His plan. Each person was created with infinite potential. When you make a mistake, stop, clear it up, and get back on track. Don't let one mistake diminish the good person you know that you are and the greatness that God knows you can achieve.

❧ *Diary of Rememberance* ❧

Record here memories of how your loved one looked at others. Did he or she give others the benefit of the doubt? Did he or she make an effort to judge others favorably? How would you describe his or her own sense of self-worth? Try to remember a story from your loved one's life that illustrates these ideas.

Our Merciful God in Heaven—May this portion of Torah learning be a merit and a blessing for my [relationship], [name]. *May* [his/her] *soul be bound in the bond of life. May* [his/her] *resting place be that of peace.*

How We Are Judged

May God remember my [relationship], [name], *in whose merit I am now studying about my heritage of Judaism and the Torah.*

We often make the mistake in our religious lives of thinking that unless we do everything perfectly, we'd be better not to do anything at all. After all, we think, why be a hypocrite?

If you attended one of my classes, "How to Raise a *Mensch*," you would hear me mention that you should never punish your children in a state of anger. Now suppose that I invite you to my home the Friday night following the class. You come to enjoy a nice Shabbat meal, but during the course of the evening my children really begin to act up. (Yes, even the Rabbi's children misbehave.) I try to patiently discipline them, distract them, bribe them, and then I lose my temper. Seething with anger, I punish them.

On the way home, you say to yourself, "Is she ever a hypocrite! Just this week she taught us that you should never punish out of anger, and tonight she did just that."

Am I a hypocrite? Hypocrites say something and do not put it into action because they never believed it in the first place. When I said that you shouldn't punish with anger, I believed it. The fact that I lost my temper on Friday night does not make me a hypocrite; it makes me a human being who is trying to live my beliefs as well as I can.

If I make a mistake raising my children, do I say, "Oh no! I lost my temper. I guess I'd better give them to the neighbor to raise"? No. I calm down, try to smooth things over, and start again.

If you're on a diet and you sneak a donut, is it right to say, "I might as well eat the whole box?" Definitely not.

24

Yet when it comes to Judaism, we often say that if we can't do it all, we might as well not do any of it. This idea is a mistake. Every mitzvah that we do, every recognition of God is forever—even if we err the second before and the second after.[11] Sometimes in life, you may take three steps forward and two steps back. But at least you're making progress!

We have our ideals—not to yell at our children, to greet everyone with a smile, to judge people kindly, to remember there is a God above us—but it's hard to live up to them. God understands that. He created us. He is not surprised when we make mistakes.

Our sages say, "According to the pain is the reward."[12] This means the reward is for trying, not accomplishing. All God wants is for us to make the effort, whether we succeed or not. God doesn't expect perfection, but He does expect us to try to understand life, to make decisions based on our values and not on whims and feelings, and to strive to live with those decisions.

Our sages ask, "What is the difference between a good person and a wicked person?" The answer: a good person falls seven times, a wicked person only once.[13] A good person falls and then gets back up, again and again and again. But a wicked person falls and never gets up.

Making mistakes cannot be avoided. What we learn from those mistakes and how we live our lives afterward is the true test of every human being.

❧ *Diary of Rememberance* ❧

You loved the person who passed away, but like every person, he or she made mistakes in life. How did your loved one react to his or her mistakes? What can you learn from this? Does a particular incident stand out in your mind? Record your thoughts here.

Our Merciful God in Heaven—May this portion of Torah learning be a merit and a blessing for my [relationship], [name]. May [his/her] soul be bound in the bond of life. May [his/her] resting place be that of peace.

Seeking Knowledge

May God remember my [relationship], [name], in whose merit I am now studying about my heritage of Judaism and the Torah.

We make a mistake in Jewish learning when we think that it is better to avoid learning about something if we don't intend to put it into practice. Why should we learn about Shabbat, we think, if we don't intend to observe Shabbat? We'll be more culpable in the eyes of God, so it's best not to know about it at all.

In fact, it's better to know and not to do than never to know at all. It's better to have knowledge, even if we aren't going to put it into practice.[14]

Imagine you have a brother who has ruined his life. His marriage has fallen apart; his children want nothing to do with him. He embezzled his partner's money, destroying his business and landing him in jail. Even in prison he managed to continue his drinking and drug habits. He's been out of jail for over six months, but he has turned into a recluse. He won't answer your phone calls and refuses to see anyone.

What do you do? He's your brother and you love him, so you march over to his apartment and demand to be let in. At first there's no response, but you keep ringing the buzzer and pleading with him to give you a chance.

Eventually you hear shuffling inside, and at last he unlocks the door. You have to hold back a gasp because you can't believe this is your brother. He's dirty, unshaven, and as thin as a rail. His apartment is a pigsty, with old moldy newspapers piled everywhere. You barely recognize him.

You remain calm, sit him down, and say, "I love you. I want to help you. I've done some research. Here's the number of Alcoholics Anonymous; they'll help you with your drinking problem. And here's the number of a hospital where people can kick their drug habits. I talked to your wife, and she's willing to reconcile; here's the number of a marriage counselor. I also spoke to your children. They are willing to talk. Here are their numbers." And you hand him a piece of paper with all the telephone numbers.

Your brother can now do one of three things. He can tear up the paper and throw it in your face, shouting, "Get out of here! I'm sorry I ever let you in!"

Or he can take the paper, put it on the table beside him, and say, "Thank you. I'm not ready to make these calls, but thank you." Or he can immediately make the calls.

Which scenario is best for him? Obviously, immediately making the calls would be best. But if he can't do that yet, the next best choice is the second, by which he thanks you and sets the paper aside. What is the difference between the first choice, by which he throws the paper in your face, and the second? In both cases he has not lifted a finger to dial even one number, but clearly, taking the information, even if he doesn't use it, is far better than rejecting it.

Our sages say that learning leads to doing, but doing doesn't always lead to learning. Knowledge can lead to action.[15] Never be afraid of knowledge. Our entire religion is based on learning and understanding. The first of the Ten Commandments is to know that there is a God. Knowledge is active: it requires information gathering, seeking, and questioning.

Imagine it's Friday night. The rabbi sees two Jewish neighbors getting into a car to drive to a ball game. He greets them, "Good *Shabbos, Shabbat Shalom!*" and asks if they want to learn about Shabbat. One says, "No thank you, I'll miss the pregame warmup." The other says, "Sure, I'd like to learn." To his friend he says, "You go ahead and I'll meet you there."

So one man drives off and the other stays and sits down for an hour while the rabbi explains the beauty and wisdom of Shabbat. The man is grateful. "Thank you, Rabbi," he says. "That was beautiful. *Shabbat Shalom*." And off he drives in time for the first pitch.

Which man is better off? They both drove and spent Friday night at the ballpark. Neither one stayed to make Kiddush over wine, but clearly the man who learned is steps ahead of the one who didn't, even if he never puts the information into practice. One day he may. But even if he doesn't, God wants him to have the knowledge.

Knowledge is empowering. And it's never too late to learn.

∂ *Diary of Rememberance* ℘

What one piece of knowledge or wisdom did your loved one give to you? Was it taught with words or by example? How has this knowledge affected your life?

_____

_____

_____

_____

_____

_____

_____

_____

_____

Our Merciful God in Heaven—May this portion of Torah learning be a merit and a blessing for my [relationship], [name]. May [his/her] soul be bound in the bond of life. May [his/her] resting place be that of peace.

The Purpose of Creation

May God remember my [relationship], [name], *in whose merit I am now studying about my heritage of Judaism and the Torah.*

Why did God create us? Perhaps it was so that we would serve Him.

As my rabbi says, if you want children in order to have them serve you, get an English butler; butlers are cheaper. God is our Father in Heaven. He didn't create us in order for us to serve Him.

Then why were we created?

People wonder about the greatness afforded to the Jewish people because we brought monotheism to the world: *Shema Yisrael, Hashem Elokeinu, Hashem Echad*—Hear O Israel, the Lord is God, God, the One and Only.

Why is monotheism the foundation of the Jewish religion? In the answer lies the purpose of creation itself. A god of the sun, a god of the moon, and a god of the stars: each one has certain attributes. But gods who rule over one thing and not another must also lack certain powers. Believers worship them and offer gifts to them according to their needs.

The existence of one God and no other means that nothing is lacking. You can't give anything to one God because He has everything. If He has no needs, He can't take. He can only give. Therefore, everything that is here is here for us, for our pleasure.[16]

Yes, we were created to experience pleasure. My rabbi calls it the biggest secret in the world. When the first man and woman were created, God put them in Gan Eden (the Garden of Eden). *Eden* means "pleasure". Our first home was the Garden of Pleasure. Later, according to the book of Genesis, God told Abraham to "go for yourself," to leave his land for another place that God would show him. Rashi, the foremost commentator on the Torah (the Five Books of Moses), explains that God is telling Abraham, "go for your pleasure; go for your own benefit."[17]

Rabbi Moshe Chayim Luzzato, the great eighteenth-century scholar, says in his book, *Path of the Just*, that we should all ask ourselves, "What am I living for?" And he says the answer is "to take pleasure in God and pleasure in His presence." That is the true pleasure, the greatest pleasure. We are all seeking it, and it can be found.

But if we were created for pleasure, how is it that our lives are filled with such struggle and pain?

If I were to ask people, "What is the opposite of pain?" Most would answer, "Pleasure." But is it? Ask parents what their greatest pleasure is, and they will probably answer, "Our children." What is their greatest source of pain? Their children!

The opposite of pain is not pleasure, it is no pain; comfort. Our greatest and deepest pleasures in life require pain and effort: marriage, children, community work, degrees, jobs, personal and spiritual growth. All of these are hard work, but realizing one's potential is one of the greatest pleasures imaginable.

❧ Diary of Rememberance ❧

What gave your loved one a sense of deep and lasting pleasure? How was it sought? What was his or her most meaningful pleasure?

_____

_____

_____

_____

_____

_____

_____

_____

_____

_____

_____

Our Merciful God in Heaven—May this portion of Torah learning be a merit and a blessing for my [relationship], [name]. May [his/her] soul be bound in the bond of life. May [his/her] resting place be that of peace.

Day Five

Who Is God?

May God remember my [relationship], [name], *in whose merit I am now studying about my heritage of Judaism and the Torah.*

Some people believe in the concept of God as Creator: He created the world but then stepped back and let it run its course. Others believe in God as Creator and Sustainer: He created the world and sustains it each and every day. The ongoing existence of the world is totally dependent upon God.

The Jewish view is threefold: Creator, Sustainer, and Supervisor. This means that God created the world, sustains it each and every day, and is personally involved with every aspect, every person, and every creation every second of the day.[18] This sounds impressive, but it also sounds a little unreal. How can it be that God is intimately involved in the lives of every person, including you and me? After all, there are over a billion people in China alone! Does God really have the time to care about each little life?

If you were one of tens of thousands of employees working at IBM, do you think the CEO would ever forget you? Of course he would! He doesn't even know you exist.

What if the CEO was your father? Would he forget you? Never. Not only would he know who you were, he would take a special interest in how you were doing and what your worries and concerns were. He would always have a hand in your life, sometimes overtly and sometimes behind the scenes. He would try to arrange (again, sometimes behind the scenes) that your work would go smoothly for you. And when necessary, he would give you a tough assignment if he knew it was for your good. Your daily progress would be carefully watched and lovingly monitored. As your father, he would want only what is best for you.

God is our Father in Heaven. Each one of us is His child.[19] He created us, gave us our parents, and brought people and events into our lives for a reason. He watches over us with love. And He doesn't forget us.

We tend to make mistakes in understanding our relationship with God because we are human and look at life through human eyes. To even begin to understand God, we have to try to break out of our limited perceptions and reach a whole different level of awareness.

We are human. God is not human. He is God. He is not male and not female but has attributes that we associate with males and females.[20] We are limited. God is unlimited. He is not restrained by the physical world, and He has the ability to make anything happen.

We are bound by time but God is beyond time. We live in the present, reflect on the past, and worry about the future. God is above time, seeing past, present, and future in one glance. He knows what happened in the past, sees us in the present, and knows the future. He is continually guiding us through life.[21]

Imagine a person in a maze. At one end is the entrance. On the other is the exit. Now imagine that the maze has no roof and we can look down and see the entire structure. We can see where the person is, where she has come from, and where she is going.

We watch as she enters and begins to move through the maze. At one point, she comes to a split. Her choice is to go left or to go right. If she turns left, she will have a clear path to the exit. If she turns right, she will come to a dead end. What she sees from her point of view is very limited, while from our vantage point, the situation is much clearer.

You've probably figured out by now that we are the ones in life's maze, and the one looking down from above is God. God looks down, sees where we are, from where we have come, and where we are going. Not only did He create us, but He also created the maze. Each person's maze is designed individually, as He puts all of life's choices before us.

If the person goes right instead of left she will hit a dead end. At that point she can do one of two things: sit down and give up or realize she's made a mistake, stop, turn around, and head back the other way, eventually finding her way to the exit.

God wants us to make the proper choices. So He brings people, events, and circumstances into our lives to help us do just that. Sometimes we get the message, sometimes not. For our person in the maze, everything possible is done to show her that she should turn left: the way is made brighter, more accessible, more inviting. Perhaps she was taught that left is best. Maybe someone else—a teacher, a mentor, is brought into her life to show her the way.

However, in order for us to understand the message that God is sending, we have to be aware that He is sending a message, that life isn't just a series of coincidences. When events happen, they happen for a reason. This is God's way of communicating with us. But remember, you can ask others for advice and guidance but in the end only you know what God is telling you. The same experience can happen to two different people and deliver two different messages. Sometimes we don't know what the message is at the moment, but with time and careful thought, looking back, often we understand.[22]

We will not always like the message or how it arrives. Hitting a wall in life can often be painful. But the choices we make, even when the path looks like a dead end, can open up endless possibilities.

❧ *Diary of Rememberance* ❧

What kind of relationship did your loved one have with God? Were events in this world seen as chance or as happening for a reason? Try to remember an event that best illustrates these ideas.

Our Merciful God in Heaven—May this portion of Torah learning be a merit and a blessing for my [relationship], [name]. *May* [his/her] *soul be bound in the bond of life. May* [his/her] *resting place be that of peace.*

What Is the Torah? — Introduction

May God remember my [relationship], [name], *in whose merit I
am now studying about my heritage of Judaism and the Torah.*

All of Judaism has as its source the giving of the Torah to Moses and the entire Jewish nation at Mount Sinai over 3,300 years ago. God spoke, and all heard. This national revelation is the unique claim of the Jewish people. As a nation, we accepted the Torah because God Himself spoke directly to the entire Jewish people, not just Moses.[23]

A story tells of a great Chassidic Rebbe who died and left three sons. The question was, which one of the sons would become the new Rebbe? A day passed. The oldest son told his brothers that, amazingly, the night before their father had come to him in a dream to tell him that he was to be the new Rebbe. The other sons were not impressed. They were still not sure who would be the new Rebbe, but it was clear that their brother certainly would not.

"If our father wanted you to be the Rebbe," said the other two sons, "he would have come to us in a dream to tell us."

The Jewish people did not simply accept the word of Moses. God spoke to the entire nation and told us to believe in Moses as a prophet.

That remarkable encounter between God and the Jewish people changed the world for all time. All the major Western religions are based on this revelation at Mount Sinai: Judaism, Christianity, and Islam all accept it as fact.

The Torah is known to the world as the Five Books of Moses, but to us it is simply the Torah. It is the Written Law, which contains the 613 commandments (*mitzvot*)—not just ten but 613. They include keeping kosher and observing Shabbat but also "Love your neighbor," "Don't bear a grudge," and the many laws that govern relationships between people.

Also given at Mount Sinai was the Oral Torah, which is less well known to most of us. We will be learning about this on another day.

TORAH, *CHUMASH,* AND TALMUD

Torah, Chumash, and *Talmud.* These are terms we hear growing up as Jews, but often we are confused as to what they are, how they relate to each other, and what they have to do with our lives today. The next four days of study will be devoted to gaining a basic understanding of what these important Jewish terms mean.

As the Jewish people wandered through the desert toward the Land of Israel, God dictated the entire Five Books (in Hebrew known as the *Chumash* from the word *chamaish,* meaning "five"), and Moses set them down. The *Chumash* begins with the creation of the world and ends with the death of Moses.

The word *Torah* means "instructions" or "teachings." It is not just a history of the Jewish people. It is referred to as *Torat Chaim,* "Instructions for Living." It is about life. Everything is in the Torah. It is about birth, death, love, marriage, sexuality, medical ethics, business—everything! It is God's guidebook for us so that we can get the most out of life, the most pleasure life has to offer. It is packed with wisdom for life—for life today. You have only to read it to receive the wisdom from it.

The problem is that most of us have never read it. (Remember that the book is always better than the movie.)

Our Merciful God in Heaven—May this portion of Torah learning be a merit and a blessing for my [relationship], [name]. *May* [his/her] *soul be bound in the bond of life. May* [his/her] *resting place be that of peace.*

What Is the Torah?
—The Five Books of Moses

May God remember my [relationship], [name], in whose merit I am now studying about my heritage of Judaism and the Torah.

I n order to begin to grasp what is in the Torah, let us quickly review what the Five Books contain.

BOOK 1: GENESIS *(IN HEBREW, BERASHIT)*

The first book contains the fundamental understanding of how we relate to God. It begins, "In the beginning . . ." with the creation of the world. We then witness the creation of the first person, Adam.

We read about Noah and the story of the ark and the flood. Next we are introduced to our forefathers and foremothers, beginning with Abraham (Avraham Avinu, the father of the Jewish people). From Abraham and his wife, Sarah, comes Isaac (Yitzhak). Isaac marries Rebecca (Rivkah). From Isaac and Rebecca comes Jacob (Yaakov). He marries Rachel and Leah. From their children will come the Twelve Tribes of Israel. They are Reuven, Shimon, Levi, Yehudah, Zevulun, Yisachar, Dan, Gad, Asher, Naphtali, Yosef, and Binyamin.

In all of Genesis, only three of the 613 *mitzvot* (commandments) are given: "Be fruitful and multiply" (the commandment to have children), *brit milah* (ritual circumcision for boys), and "Don't eat the vein from the flank of meat" (found in the story of Jacob wrestling with an angel). The rest of Genesis contains stories and narratives that teach us lessons we can apply to our lives today.

BOOK 2: EXODUS *(SHEMOT)*

The second book is about the enslavement of the Jewish people in Egypt and their eventual redemption and exodus. In Exodus we are introduced to Moses (Moshe). We learn of the oppression of the Jewish people in Egypt and of the famous burning bush encounter when God comes to Moses and tells him that he will lead the Jews out of Egypt. (This may sound familiar not only because of the movie *The Ten Commandments* but also from the Passover Seder.) We also meet Aaron, the older brother of Moses.

In Egypt the ten plagues descend, ending with the death of the firstborn. The first Passover Seder is held, and the Jews at last go free, traveling through the desert on their way to Mount Sinai.

After leaving Egypt and crossing the Red Sea, the Jewish people encamp at Mount Sinai, where God reveals Himself to the nation and through Moses gives them the tablets of the Ten Commandments and all the rest of the 613 *mitzvot* of the Torah. They are told to build the Tabernacle (Mishkan), which is the mobile sanctuary that will be carried with them during the years in the desert. In it will be housed the tablets of the Ten Commandments. And it is there that God's presence will dwell the strongest.

The Book of Exodus recounts the birth of the Jewish people as a nation, for only at the moment of receiving the Torah were we truly united.

BOOK 3: LEVITICUS *(VA'YIKRA)*

In Leviticus we have a break in the narrative, with almost the entire book dedicated to the concept of holiness. Sacrifices in the Mishkan are discussed in detail. Many laws are provided, including the dietary laws of *kashrut*, laws of sexuality, and special days such as Shabbat (the Sabbath), Rosh Hashanah, Yom Kippur, and Sukkot.

Other commandments in this book include "Love your neighbor," "Don't bear a grudge," and "Don't take revenge."

BOOK 4: NUMBERS *(BAMIDBAR)*

The book of Numbers tells the story of the years that the Jewish people spent in the desert on their journey to the Land of Israel. Now the Jewish people are living as a community.

A census is taken among the tribes, and the Land of Israel (which the people have yet to enter as a nation) is divided, with a portion allocated for each tribe. But not all is well as the Jewish people meet the challenges of living under Torah law. Miriam, the sister of Moses, errs by speaking *lashon hara* (gossip, evil speech) and is punished. A power struggle erupts among the Jews, with a rebellion led by Korach. It is put down, and Korach is punished. Miriam and Aaron both die, and war is fought with enemies along the way. Moses is told to prepare for his death, as he will not merit entering the Land of Israel because of a mistake he made in carrying out God's orders.

Commandments in this book include laws of speech, justice, and marriage.

BOOK 5: DEUTERONOMY *(DEVARIM)*

The events in the final book of the Torah take place during the last thirty-seven days of the life of Moses. Moses knows he is going to die and takes this time to give the Jewish people their final instructions and his predictions of what will happen in the future if they make certain choices. Most importantly, he pleads with them to take the Torah to heart. He reviews everything they have been through together: slavery, freedom, revelation, rebellions, and God's miracles.

Deuteronomy is about taking all that the Jewish people have learned so far and internalizing it. Various laws are reviewed, including the Ten Commandments. And here we are given the Shema, the Jewish credo that states, "Hear O Israel, the Lord is God, the Lord is One." We are warned against assimilation, idolatry, and character flaws such as arrogance and stubbornness.

At the very end of the book, Moses delivers his final heartfelt words to the people, and then his disciple, Joshua, is appointed as his successor to lead the Jewish people into the Land of Israel. Moses gives his final blessings to each of the twelve tribes. At last, at the end of the Torah, Moses dies.

For Further Reading

Rabbi Aryeh Kaplan, *The Living Torah* (New York: Maznaim Publishing, 1981); Rabbi Nosson Scherman, *The Stone Chumash* (New York: Artscroll-Mesorah Publications, 2006); Rabbi Zelig Pliskin, *Growth Through Torah* (New York: Benei Yakov Publications, 1988); J. S. Hahn, *Bible Basics* (New York: Feldheim, 1997); Rabbi Nachum Braverman, *Bible for the Clueless but Curious* (Baltimore: Leviathan Press, 1999).

Our Merciful God in Heaven—May this portion of Torah learning be a merit and a blessing for my [relationship], [name]. *May* [his/her] *soul be bound in the bond of life. May* [his/her] *resting place be that of peace.*

Day Eight

What Is the Torah? — The Oral Torah

May God remember my [relationship], [name], *in whose merit I am now studying about my heritage of Judaism and the Torah.*

Until this point we have discussed the Written Torah, which is the Five Books of Moses. But additional instructions were given at Mount Sinai, which we call the Oral Torah. [24] Why were additional instructions given, and why were they given orally?

If you go to a class and take notes, and a friend who misses the class asks to borrow your notes, will he understand the whole class from them? Unless he discusses the class with you at length, he will miss a good deal of it.

The Written Torah is the class notes, and the Oral Torah is the discussion. All of the 613 commandments appear in the Written Torah, but none of them could be understood and carried out without further explanation. We are told to affix *mezuzahs* to our doorposts. What is a *mezuzah*? What does it contain? Where should it be placed on the doorpost? Should every doorpost have one? We are told to put on *tefillin*. What are they? What do they contain? What color, shape, and size are they? I am supposed to honor my parents. How does one do that? What are my obligations to care for them if they are sick or elderly? What if I don't like them? What if they neglected their duties to me? We are told not to murder, but what about self-defense or capital punishment? Did God leave these decisions to our personal opinions?

I think you get the idea. It's not enough to say, "Put a *mezuzah* on your doorpost." Further instructions are clearly in order.

In the Written Torah, we see references to an additional set of instructions. One example is in the book of Deuteronomy (12:21), when God is giving the laws of *kashrut*. He says, "You shall slaughter your cattle . . . as I have commanded you." But if you look from one end of the Written Torah to the other, you will find no instructions on how to slaughter animals. This is because when the text says, "as I have commanded you," it is referring to a set of instructions that was given orally and not as part of the Written Torah. So if you want to find out how a Jew slaughters animals in a prescribed kosher manner, you must look to the Oral Torah, and not to the Written Torah.[25]

The purpose of the Oral Torah was to add a dynamic, living dimension to the Torah. If the law was oral, we would need teachers. The oral laws would have to be passed down from person to person. The discussions about it would keep it alive.[26]

But wasn't the message garbled along the way as in the old game of telephone? In telephone someone makes up a message, and it is passed along from person to person until the final person announces a usually very confused and nonsensical version of the original message.

Consider this scenario instead: You are on vacation at a cottage, when suddenly you hear shouting from near the water. Someone is yelling for help. "Call the hospital! Someone has fallen in the water and we're trying to revive him!"

You immediately call the hospital. You are asked to describe the situation and to report on the victim's vital signs. You ask someone in the cottage to relay the questions down to the beach. They are shouted from person to person, and the answers come back in the same fashion. When they finally reach you, you report them over the phone to the hospital. Back and forth the information travels until the ambulance arrives or the person is no longer in danger.

Why aren't we worried this time that the information might have become distorted along the way? Because each person in the chain knows that every word means the difference between life and death.

When God spoke at Mount Sinai and gave us critical wisdom for physical and spiritual life, we listened. And when He told us to pass it down, teacher to student, parent to child, we did just that. Every word counted. It was not a game; it was life itself.

45

The Oral Torah was written down between 150 and 180 C.E., after the destruction of the Second Temple in Jerusalem. The destruction of the Second Temple created enormous and horrific upheaval in Jewish society. The Romans conquered the Jewish people, many leading sages were murdered, many of the great academies and schools were disbanded, thousands of Jews were enslaved, and almost the entire population of Israel was forced into exile. Chaos reigned. The leading rabbis of the time saw that the upheaval caused by the exile posed a serious threat to the integrity of the smooth transmission of the Oral Torah. These threats led to the written codification of the Oral Torah called the Mishna, compiled by Rabbi Judah the Prince, the preeminent scholar of the time.[27]

Our Merciful God in Heaven—May this portion of Torah learning be a merit and a blessing for my [relationship], [name]. May [his/her] soul be bound in the bond of life. May [his/her] resting place be that of peace.

What Is the Torah? — The Talmud

May God remember my [relationship], [name], *in whose merit I am now studying about my heritage of Judaism and the Torah.*

After the exile discussed yesterday, the center of Jewish life was no longer in Jerusalem, but in Iraq (known then as Babylon). The Gemorah, also referred to as the Talmud, is the discussion and abstract analysis of the Mishna (Oral Torah) written between the years 200 and 500 C.E. The Talmud is written in Aramaic, which was the spoken language of the Jews in Iraq. It is the storehouse of ethics, philosophy, and law, dealing with every aspect of a person's life.

The two negative stereotypes you hear about the Talmud are (1) the sages are always arguing, and (2) it is filled with nitpicky details. They are both true. But the sages are arguing over the details of about 1 percent of law; the other 99 percent of it they accept in total agreement.

Here is an example: The Talmud contains lengthy discussions about the laws relating to the marriage ceremony. The sages all agree that to make the union binding under Jewish law, the man has to give something of value to the woman, and she has to agree to accept it for the purpose of marriage. Two witnesses must see this transaction take place. Today this is done under the *chuppah* (marriage canopy) with the giving of the ring.

A dispute arises in the Talmud regarding the minimum value of the ring. Will a ring from a bubble gum machine do? Must it have a diamond, and if so, how big? The school of thought that followed Rabbi Hillel said that the minimum acceptable value was approximately five cents, whereas Rabbi Shamai said it must be at least five dollars. Both schools of thought agree that something of value has to be given, that both parties must consent to the marriage, that witnesses must be present, and both agree that five dollars is acceptable. The argument therefore is whether the value can be as low as five cents.[28] (If I were the bride, I would be pretty annoyed either way.)[29]

TANACH

Tanach is an acronym that stands for Torah/Neviim/Ketuvim. The Torah is the Five Books of Moses we've discussed over the last two days.

Neviim is the Books of the Prophets. Thousands of years ago, there were many prophets, but in Tanach only those are included who have messages for all time, such as Isaiah and Jeremiah. Included are the accounts of King David and King Solomon and other great leaders of the Jewish people. To read and study them is to learn vital messages from God, which speak to us today.

Prophets can be men or women, but they are only considered prophets if they
- Possess great wisdom
- Are of the highest moral character
- Have *simcha* (joy)[30]
- Are specific, not general, in their prophetic predictions
- Make predictions that come true at least three times

People are also declared to be prophets by another prophet (as Moses declared of Joshua).[31]

Neviim contains no laws, only ethical teachings.[32] These books cover about 800 years of the history of the Jewish people, beginning with their entrance into the Land of Israel (the Book of Joshua).

Ketuvim is the books of Writings. These additional books convey deep and beautiful messages. They include famous works such as Psalms (*Tehillim*), many written by King David; Proverbs (*Mishlei*), written by King Solomon; the Book of Ruth (*Megillat Ruth*), which is read at Shavuot; the Book of Esther (*Megillat Esther*), which is read at Purim; and Ecclesiastes (*Kohelet*), written by King Solomon and read during the holiday of Sukkot.

 For Further Reading

Rabbi Nosson Scherman, *The Artscroll Tanach*, (New York: Artscroll-Mesorah Publications, 1996).

Our Merciful God in Heaven—May this portion of Torah learning be a merit and a blessing for my [relationship], [name]. *May* [his/her] *soul be bound in the bond of life. May* [his/her] *resting place be that of peace.*

Kaddish

May God remember my [relationship]*,* [name]*, in whose merit I am now studying about my heritage of Judaism and the Torah.*

"Yitgadal v'yitkadash sh'mei rabbaw."
May His great name grow exalted and sanctified.

"Y'hei sh'mei rabbaw m'vawrach l'allum u'l'allmei allmayaw."
May His great Name be blessed forever and ever.

We have already learned that the soul of a person lives on after death and that what we do here in this world can affect the person beyond. When we act in someone's memory, we increase his or her portion of pleasure in the World to Come.

When we stand and say the mourner's Kaddish, we are praising God.[33] Why? To praise God in times of joy is easy. To praise Him in times of sorrow is much harder.[34] Kaddish is the recognition that He has an ultimate plan for the world, that every individual has a unique role to play in that plan, and that the plan is good.

Remembering a loved one in this way is a statement that the special relationship between you has dramatically changed. In this world, you enjoyed a relationship of give and take. Now that your loved one is in the next world, you can only give.

With Kaddish, we praise God because He is now the vital link in this new relationship. When you remember your loved one, it means his or her presence here made a difference and continues to make a difference as you are inspired to continue the relationship through your deeds and actions.

Kaddish brings God closer in this world. It is said with others to collectively affirm our relationship with our Creator. At the same time, saying it is lifting the soul of the departed one closer to God. The Almighty is the point of linkage between us and our departed loved ones.

When you say Kaddish, you are affirming a new awareness of God that has grown out of your relationship with the person in whose memory you are saying Kaddish. Kaddish is one of the ways, along with studying the Torah, giving charity, performing meritorious deeds in your loved one's name, accepting more Jewish involvement and commitment, and so on, in which you can make a real difference for someone for eternity.

Another way to remember is by naming a child after the loved one. Our tradition tells us that a spark of that person will live on in the child and that the child will embody some of the special qualities of that person.[35] This special honor is a genuine merit to the person who passed away and can make a difference for them in the World to Come.

WHO SAYS KADDISH?

A direct mourner says Kaddish for a loved one who has passed away.[36] You are considered a direct mourner if you have lost a parent, spouse, sibling, or child. A person says Kaddish for a parent for eleven months during daily services (held three times per day) where there is a *minyan* (a quorum of ten men), present. For all others, Kaddish is said for only thirty days. If you are unable to fulfill your obligation of saying Kaddish, you can arrange to sponsor someone to do it on your behalf. Your local Yeshiva or synagogue will surely help you make the arrangements.

For Further Reading

Rabbi Nosson Sherman, *Kaddish* (New York: Artscroll-Mesorah, 1991).

✆ *Diary of Rememberance* ✆

If you are saying Kaddish, or have said it, record here your feelings about the process. Do your feelings change as time goes on? What is the connection between you, your loved one, and the prayer itself? How do you feel, or did you feel, walking into synagogue, saying Kaddish, and then walking out?

_____

_____

_____

_____

_____

_____

_____

_____

_____

_____

_____

Our Merciful God in Heaven—May this portion of Torah learning be a merit and a blessing for my [relationship], [name]. *May* [his/her] *soul be bound in the bond of life. May* [his/her] *resting place be that of peace.*

Laws of Speech — Lashon Hara

May God remember my [relationship], [name], in whose merit I am now studying about my heritage of Judaism and the Torah.

Judge your people fairly. Do not go around as a gossiper among your people. (Leviticus 19:15-16)

The Talmud says that speech is where the body and soul meet. A human being is actually described as a "speaking soul" when man is created in the book of Genesis.[37] The gift of speech can be an instrument for enormous good: an inspiring talk can move millions, positive words can build a child's self-esteem, words of love can unite a man and a woman for eternity. But used in another way, speech has the power to destroy.

The laws of speech are referred to as the laws of lashon hara, literally "evil speech." For just as words can build and inspire, when used in a destructive manner they can bring evil to the world.

WHY PEOPLE SPEAK *LASHON HARA*

The basis for lashon hara is arrogance. Belittling others gives one a feeling of self-importance. This in turn creates a false and empty sense of self-worth that can damage the speaker even more than the one the speaker has chosen to put down.

Think for a moment of the wisdom that went into the creation of every person. We were given two ears to hear with, two nostrils to smell with, but just one mouth. In addition, God made the mouth so that it can close on its own. The message is clear: There are times to talk, and there are times to be silent. But how do we know the difference?

The Oral Torah discusses when we are forbidden to speak about others and when we are obligated to do so. It says that gossiping and speaking badly about someone "kills" three people.[38] The first victim is the person spoken badly about, because people now view that person in a negative light; someone's reputation has been blemished forever. The second victim is the speaker because although a person gets a tremendous amount of attention when relaying gossip, in the long run, that person is not one that others will confide in. Clearly the gossiper is not trustworthy and gains pleasure from putting others down. When we speak destructively about others, we not only victimize someone but we also affect our closeness to God. Speaking in a manner that is hurtful to others diminishes us spiritually. The ability to think and speak is a gift meant to be used to elevate people, not to destroy them.

And lastly, the Talmud says that the person who is the most culpable is the listener. Why is the listener transgressing the most? Because we are not supposed to speak lashon hara, and we are not supposed to listen to lashon hara. And the listener is the most capable of putting a stop to it all.

How does one stop listening to lashon hara? Suppose you are at a party, and you walk over to a group of people who are involved in an animated conversation. As you approach, you realize the topic of the night is a couple you know who isn't there. The best thing to do is to keep on walking and find someone else to socialize with.

Sometimes it's not that easy to avoid gossip. Imagine you are already standing with a group of people, and the conversation takes a negative turn. If you can't exit gracefully, the best thing is to try to tactfully suggest that the group shouldn't be talking like this. (This suggestion is not always cheerfully received.)

Another tactic is to quickly try to change the topic. ("Hey, did you hear that So-and-So had a baby?") If the person or group doesn't get the hint and keeps coming back to the gossip, then try to show how the negative story might have another side to it. Point out something positive about the person being spoken about or a plausible reason for the situation. ("You may think she is a snob, but I hear she is just painfully shy.")

However, putting a positive spin on a story may not be accepted by a person or group determined to speak badly about others. When all else fails—when you are unable to exit, when everyone else refuses to grant someone the benefit of the doubt, and when you can't change the topic of discussion—then what you have to do is not believe what is being said.[39]

In your mind you have to say, "I don't believe this," and think about all the reasons the story couldn't be true. After all, there is always another side to a story. How many times have people misjudged something you have said or done?

One is not allowed to speak badly about other people.[40] In addition, one is not allowed to speak badly about organizations, groups of people, or even the Land of Israel.[41]

Based on what we've just learned, you might think that it's best to only speak positively about people. That's a good start, but even then we must be careful. If you know that David is envious of Jim's wealth, no mitzvah is accomplished in running to David to talk about Jim's latest purchase or large charitable contribution. This can only spark negative rhetoric and lashon hara.[42]

Suppose you tell your sister-in-law how helpful your mother is, how she is at your house with the children day and night, and how you have plans to attend the theater together. Be aware that this may cause your sister-in-law to wonder why she doesn't get this kind of attention. All the positive talk about your mother may cause bad feelings.

As you can see, careful speech demands great sensitivity.

For Further Reading

Michael Rothschild, Rabbi Shimon Finkelman, *Chofetz Chaim: A Daily Companion* (New York: Artscroll-Mesorah, 1999); Lori Palatnik, *Gossip: Ten Pathways to Eliminate It from Your Life and Transform Your Soul* (Deerfield Beach: Simcha Press, 2002).

❧ *Diary of Rememberance* ❧

Tomorrow we will discuss the times you are allowed to speak of others. In the meantime, try and think about how your loved one used the gift of speech. Can you remember a time when his or her words made a difference for someone? Perhaps it was for you. Write down what happened.

_____

_____

_____

_____

_____

_____

_____

_____

_____

_____

Our Merciful God in Heaven—May this portion of Torah learning be a merit and a blessing for my [relationship], [name]. *May* [his/her] *soul be bound in the bond of life. May* [his/her] *resting place be that of peace.*

Laws of Speech — Permitted Speech

May God remember my [relationship]*,* [name]*, in whose merit I am now studying about my heritage of Judaism and the Torah.*

A good rule to always follow is to think before you talk. It's clear that negative talk and gossip are hateful and wasted words that should be avoided at all costs. But to decide when saying something positive could be interpreted as negative, you must be sensitive to the people you are speaking to and about.

You may speak if there is some benefit in what you are saying; for example, when you are trying to help someone else. Running home and telling your husband that the So-and-Sos are getting a divorce (with all the dirty details) is very different from coming home and telling him they are having trouble in their marriage and that since he is close to the husband, maybe he should try to encourage a reconciliation. In the first scenario, the conversation is idle gossip and slanderous hearsay. In the second, it's relating only what information is necessary (leaving out the dirty details) in order to help someone. It is plain what God wants from us.

It is proper to talk about someone in a negative way if a benefit is clearly intended.[43] If someone comes to you who is interested in marrying someone that you know and wants information about him or her, you must be careful what you say. You can relate specific and necessary information, but you should try and present it in an unbiased way. (Just the fact that you don't like him doesn't mean she shouldn't either.) This also applies to a business partnership.

If you must discuss a situation with someone, it's best to do it without using names. For example, if you just had a falling out with someone, you are allowed to seek advice from a friend regarding how to handle the problem if you try to avoid using names. People can often advise you without knowing whom you are talking about.

Speaking lashon hara about yourself is forbidden. You are created in the image of God; therefore, putting yourself down reflects negatively on God. Just as you wouldn't want your children to label themselves "stupid" or "lazy," you should not put such labels on yourself.

RATIONALIZING *LASHON HARA*

People often use excuses to speak badly about others. These are classic ones:

- "But it's true." You are not supposed to speak badly about others, whether what you say is true or not.
- "Everybody knows it." Even if the lashon hara is on the front page of the morning newspaper, that does not give you license to speak about it.
- "If she were here, I would say it to her face." The chances are you wouldn't say it to her face. But even if you would, or were given permission by the person herself, you may not speak lashon hara about her.
- "I can tell my spouse anything." The laws of lashon hara apply between husband and wife too. You can't gossip or speak badly to each other about others just because you are married. (This also applies to children. You can't speak lashon hara to your children or speak lashon hara about them.)
- "I was only joking." Every joke includes an element of truth. Jokes can hurt too.

Beyond speaking badly about someone, we are also forbidden to repeat anything that someone said unless we have permission. In the Torah, even God spoke to Moses "telling him to say" to the Jewish people something of importance. Moses needed permission to repeat the information. We may think the person doesn't care whether we repeat the news or not, but we don't know it. If someone tells you he is thinking of moving out of state, you have no right to tell someone else, even if the person didn't tell you in confidence. If he wants someone else to know his business, he will tell it himself. It is not up to you to be the messenger.

The exception to this rule is when the information is public. (Remember, this is not lashon hara but simple information). For example, if someone has had a baby, you don't need permission to tell a mutual friend the good news. (But don't forget to be sensitive to those who are struggling to have children.) Also, if someone told you personal news in front of three or more people and did not qualify it as a secret, you can assume the news is public and speak about it.

In general, it is good to err on the side of not speaking about other people's lives. We don't want people speaking about us, so we should give the same courtesy to others.

If you are known as a person who doesn't speak lashon hara, won't listen to it, and holds people's lives in confidence, not only does God look at you in great favor, but you will win the respect and loyalty of others. If everyone made an effort in this area, think about the harmony that would prevail, the peace that would remain among us, the goodwill that would be created toward others, and the healthy and secure sense of privacy we would have about life.

❧ *Diary of Rememberance* ❧

Think of another example of how your loved one used words in a positive way. What did this teach you about dealing with others?

_____

_____

_____

_____

_____

_____

_____

_____

_____

_____

_____

_____

_____

Our Merciful God in Heaven—May this portion of Torah learning be a merit and a blessing for my [relationship], [name]. *May* [his/her] *soul be bound in the bond of life. May* [his/her] *resting place be that of peace.*

Laws of Speech — Speaking the Truth

May God remember my [relationship], [name], *in whose merit I am now studying about my heritage of Judaism and the Torah.*

Truth is a very important value in Judaism, but what about the white lies that people tell? According to our sages, one is allowed to "change the truth" in three circumstances:[44]

1. For peace
2. For privacy
3. To minimize one's accomplishments

FOR PEACE

If someone has a new haircut and asks you, "How do you like it?" and you hate it, you are allowed to lie in order to spare her feelings. You can say you love it. Why? Because the haircut has already been done. By being brutally honest, telling her what you think of the haircut she already has, you are only going to cause pain, and possibly even conflict. You may lie to keep peace in her own emotions and self-image. (However, the next time she plans to get her hair cut, gently suggest that maybe she should give your own stylist a try.)

If your friends invite you over to see their newly decorated home and you walk into a house that is orange and purple from top to bottom, there is no benefit in telling them that just being there makes you nauseous. If they really wanted your opinion, they would have consulted with you before decorating. This is a time to praise their décor. Their feelings are more important than the truth.

Suppose you have two friends who are not speaking to one another. You are allowed to approach one and say that the other wants to get together and talk things over. And then you can approach the other party and say the same thing. This may indeed bring them together to patch things up. Even though you stretched the truth to create the meeting, your lie is allowed because you were doing it with the intention of creating peace.

FOR PRIVACY

The Torah respects a person's rights to privacy and personal dignity. If you are asked a question and the truthful answer would be embarrassing or violate your privacy, you may change the truth to protect yourself. This applies only in a case in which the other person has no right to ask the question. The tax agent asking your annual income has a right to a truthful answer; a curious friend does not.

It may occur to you to say, "It's none of your business!" This is not always possible with a boss, a parent, or someone who will deduce the truth from your reluctance to answer.

If you want to keep private certain aspects of your life that are no one's business but your own, you are allowed to lie in order to maintain that privacy.

TO MINIMIZE ONE'S ACCOMPLISHMENTS

If someone approaches you and says, "Congratulations on a job well done. I heard you ran that fund-raiser all by yourself!" You can answer, "Thank you, but it was really a group effort," even if you did do it all by yourself.

If you have decided to help someone anonymously and a friend inquires whether you are the one who is supporting that poor family, you are allowed to change the truth to minimize or hide what you are doing. You know what you did. God knows what you did. No one else needs to know.

❧ *Diary of Rememberance* ❧

How did your loved one value truth? Can you recall a story about it? What did this teach you?

_____

_____

_____

_____

_____

_____

_____

_____

_____

_____

_____

Our Merciful God in Heaven—May this portion of Torah learning be a merit and a blessing for my [relationship], [name]. May [his/her] soul be bound in the bond of life. May [his/her] resting place be that of peace.

Day Fourteen

Prayer—God Hears Your Prayers

May God remember my [relationship], [name], in whose merit I am now studying about my heritage of Judaism and the Torah.

People have lost touch with their relationship with God and what it means. The results are confusion and misconceptions about God and our connection to Him. You should remember three points when you pray to Him. Two are discussed in today's learning, and the third will be discussed tomorrow.

The three points are:

1. God is everywhere
2. God hears your prayers
3. You can ask Him for anything

GOD IS EVERYWHERE

I attended a seminar given by an advertising executive who had left his six-figure salary, dozens of employees, and numerous perks in order to train for and join an expedition to Mount Everest along with his twenty-one-year-old son. He shared his dramatic adventure in a slide presentation on the climb as a metaphor for achieving one's potential. I was impressed by his story.

In his quest to climb Mount Everest, this man saw mountains and vistas that can only be described as breathtaking. At one point, his son lost his footing and went sliding down the mountainside until a rock jammed between his back and his heavy pack, halting his fall. Moments that seemed like hours ticked by until a rope could be safely thrown to the son so that he could be saved.

For part of the trip they joined a team from France. One of the group's best climbers decided to go ahead of the rest, "trying to be the master of his own destiny." He perished before reaching the top. Two deaths occurred during the climb, several near deaths (including the presenter's son's), and enough awe-inspiring events to last a lifetime.

At the end of the one-hour presentation, the lights were turned on and questions were answered. Afterward, while the audience enjoyed refreshments, I approached the presenter with my own question: "You experienced life and death, saw nature at its best and worst, almost lost your own life, and almost lost your son. Did you ever once think about God?"

He turned to me, the smile on his face frozen, his eyes momentarily losing their sparkle. "No," he said. "Not once." After a moment's pause he explained that he wasn't "churchgoing." "Sometimes," he explained, "I feel more spiritual in a closet."

We can lose interest in prayer because of uninspiring experiences in our houses of worship and because we think that God only hears us when we're sitting all dressed up in rows with prayer books in our hands.

Our relationship with God does not depend on our being in synagogue. Ideally, synagogue is a place to help inspire us through communal prayer and song, but we are making a mistake if we greet God when we walk in and leave Him when we walk out the door.

God is everywhere. He is in our homes, our cars, at the bus stop, and at the top of Mount Everest.[45]

Because the mountain wasn't in a house of worship, the adventurer dismissed any feelings he had of spirituality or closeness to God. The Everest expedition should have offered him a front-row view of his Creator, but his seat had an obstructed view. His spirituality remained "in the closet" and his life and death experiences were described as luck, chance, and coincidence.

GOD HEARS YOUR PRAYERS

Prayer does not have to come from a book. Formal prayers were written to help us and guide us, not to stifle us. Some people need more structure than others, and some people enjoy the formality of set prayers. But if the prayer book is holding you back when it is in your hand, put it down and just talk to God.[46]

Prayer doesn't have to be in a particular language.[47] God understands all languages. He understands your words, and He understands your thoughts.

If you want to talk to God, talk. That is prayer. He hears every word. He wants to hear your prayers, not because He needs them—He doesn't need anything. You need your prayers.

When is the right time? When your heart is full, when you have a need, when you are confused, when you are angry, when you are thankful, or when you want to connect? Anytime is the right time. Especially now.

(Tomorrow's lesson will discuss point 3, "You Can Ask Him for Anything.")

For Further Reading

Rabbi Hayim Halevy Donin, *To Pray as a Jew* (New York: Basic Books, 1980); Shimon Apisdorf, *Rosh Hashanah Yom Kippur Survival Kit*, Chapter 12, "Six Perspectives on Prayer" (Baltimore: Leviathan Press, 1994); Rabbi Abraham J. Twerski, *Twerski on Prayer* (New York: Shaar Press, 2004); Yitzchok Kirzner and Lisa Aiken, *The Art of Jewish Prayer* (New York: Judaica Press, 2003); Rabbi Aryeh Kaplan, *Jewish Meditation: A Practical Guide* (New York: Schocken Books, 1995).

❧ *Diary of Rememberance* ❧

Do you ever renember your loved one talking about prayer? Try to recall the time and events.

_____

_____

_____

_____

_____

_____

_____

_____

_____

_____

Our Merciful God in Heaven—May this portion of Torah learning be a merit and a blessing for my [relationship], [name]. May [his/her] soul be bound in the bond of life. May [his/her] resting place be that of peace.

Prayer — You Can Ask Him for Anything

May God remember my [relationship], [name], *in whose merit I am now studying about my heritage of Judaism and the Torah.*

Two ideas seem to hold people back from a full relationship with God in prayer. One is that we shouldn't bother God with little requests, and the other is that we shouldn't ask Him for something too big.

Both ideas are incorrect.

Would you want your children to come to you only at times of great need because they thought that coming to you with small requests would annoy you? You want your children to feel comfortable about coming to you for anything, big or small. You may not always be able to fulfill their requests, but their asking helps build a loving relationship.

Is anything too great to ask God for? No. Because nothing that you can ask for is greater than what He has already given you. He gave you life, understanding, free will, and moral sensitivity. All requests pale in comparison.

Don't feel that small, day-to-day requests somehow use up your prayer quota. Asking for help in finding the car keys or getting a parking spot right in front of the bank does not take away from your relationship with God. In fact, such requests only add to it.[48]

Remember that God is not there only for cliff-hanging moments. He is there at the checkout aisle, in the classroom, in the Laundromat, and at the office. The lines are always open.

WHEN GOD ANSWERS PRAYERS

Virtually everyone prays: people who are religious, people who don't associate with any formal religion, sophisticated and educated people, and those less worldly or well read. One survey reported that over half of Americans pray every day. About half the remaining number pray weekly. In fact, of those who profess not to believe in God, one in five prays daily![49] I am quite sure that if the question was "Have you ever prayed?" a resounding "Yes" would have come from close to 100 percent.

My rabbi once asked a man who wasn't particularly religious if he ever prayed. "Rabbi," said the man, "I pray every day."

Impressed, my rabbi asked, "Tell me, did God ever answer your prayers?"

"Every day," was his emphatic answer. "Sometimes the answer was yes, and sometimes it was no."

We call out to God and He always hears. We listen and He always answers. Sometimes the answer may be painful, but somehow, because God sees our lifetime many years ahead, the answer is ultimately for our good.

This does not take away the pain of the moment and does not mean that we are not sometimes frustrated and angry with God. We are human, and it is difficult for us to understand, looking at the world in a limited, human fashion, why things happen the way they do.[50]

We must remember that the God who created us loves us more than our parents love us and more than we will ever love our children. That the pain we endure is somehow for our good is difficult to accept, especially at the time of our greatest losses. Yet we must never forget that the ones who are gone are no longer in pain, and they understand now why everything in life happened the way it did.

And they are in a world of infinite pleasure, aware of what we are doing here and hoping that our sorrow is short-lived and that we are comforted by those around us and by the knowledge that the essence of who they are, their soul, lives on forever.

❧ *Diary of Rememberance* ❧

What did you learn from your loved one about your relationship to God?

_____

_____

_____

_____

_____

_____

_____

_____

_____

_____

_____

Our Merciful God in Heaven—May this portion of Torah learning be a merit and a blessing for my [relationship], [name]. May [his/her] soul be bound in the bond of life. May [his/her] resting place be that of peace.

Day Sixteen

Shabbat

May God remember my [relationship], [name], in whose merit I am now studying about my heritage of Judaism and the Torah.

In the present day, we are witnessing something unique. All over the world, thousands of mature adults are taking a second look at what it means to be Jewish and through learning are beginning slowly to incorporate some of the beauty of their heritage into their lives. One of the first areas people approach is Shabbat. For in Shabbat is found all the beauty, depth, and wisdom of what it means to be a Jew.

The Sabbath, *Shabbos*, Shabbat. What is so important about this special day? Is it simply a day of rest or is it one of the Ten Commandments given to us by God for a more profound reason?

Shabbat does not actually mean "to rest" but rather "to cease," "to stop." On the seventh day, God stopped creating.

From Friday sundown until late Saturday evening is Shabbat. During this time we refrain from certain activities and focus on what life is all about.

On Shabbat, we take a step back and cease creating in order to recognize that we indeed have a Creator.

Throughout the week it is easy to get caught up in our accomplishments and projects. It is a natural outcome of the extremely busy lives we lead. Thus we were given a day to refocus and get back in touch with the meaning of it all and, most important, the Source of it all.

Shabbat is a time for love of God. It is a peaceful, relaxing, but above all connecting time. This is our time to relate to our Creator and all He has given us.

During Shabbat we spend time with friends and family, for it is in the home that we see the true value of Judaism and a Jewish life. We dress in our finest clothes and bring to the table our best silver and china. Our homes take on a different quality. Our actions seem more refined and purposeful. We are in touch with something greater than ourselves.

Special Shabbat services at the synagogue connect us to the community and through prayer help us to focus on our blessings.

As Shabbat approaches and the candles are lit, we begin a day that will give us all the spiritual and physical nourishment we need to grow as individuals connected to a people.

We enter Shabbat one way and we leave another. When it is over, we have learned and grown so that we can give more to our daily lives and to others.

Some people like to begin easing into the idea of observing Shabbat with Friday night, lighting candles, making Kiddush, or sharing a special meal or maybe a little song. Others try turning off the phones and the television one Shabbat a month, gradually getting a taste of the tranquility of Shabbat.

Everyone approaches the day differently, and that's okay because Shabbat is a unique experience—unique to each person. No one can tell you what you will feel and what it will add to your life because Shabbat is different for everyone.

For some, the blessing over the bread is the week's most spiritual moment, filled with thoughts of God's outstretched hand leading the Jews out of Egypt and the blessings He bestows upon us at every moment. For others, thoughts at the time are "Boy, this looks yummy!"

Both thoughts are valid. Because Shabbat is filled with so much, each individual as a unique soul has an opportunity to understand why it was, and still is, one of the foundations of the Jewish people.

Approach Shabbat one step at a time. And know that by fulfilling this commandment from God, you are bringing the light of all that He gives into your home and into your heart.

For Further Reading

Rabbi Shimon Finkelman, *Shabbos: Its Essence and Significance* (New York: Artscroll- Mesorah, 1994).

∾ *Diary of Rememberance* ↞

Plan to mark Shabbat in some special way in memory of your loved one. Write here what you plan to do. Try to link your observance to something special about your loved one. (For example: If your loved one was devoted to family, try to incorporate the special blessings one gives to children on Friday night. If it was a woman who passed away, try reciting Eishet Chayil (Song in Praise of Women) on Friday night, or making sure candles are lit to begin Shabbat.)

_____

_____

_____

_____

_____

_____

_____

_____

_____

_____

Our Merciful God in Heaven—May this portion of Torah learning be a merit and a blessing for my [relationship], [name]. *May* [his/her] *soul be bound in the bond of life. May* [his/her] *resting place be that of peace.*

The Jewish Holidays

May God remember my [relationship], [name], *in whose merit I am now studying about my heritage of Judaism and the Torah.*

In our youth and even today, the seasonal celebrations and family holiday gatherings provide a comforting reminder of our Jewish heritage and our bond with the Jewish people. But is that why we are commanded to observe these days, for comfort and historical connection? In fact there is much more to our holidays.

The cycle of the Jewish year is God's blueprint for growth. Each holiday is a special opportunity for every one of us to reexamine where we are and where we are going.[51] When we understand the message of each holiday and actively participate in the traditional observance, not only are we fulfilling an important Torah commandment, but also we grow as individuals and as a people.

Passover is more than just the anniversary of our escape from Egypt; it is the time of our freedom; not just our physical freedom, but a freedom that we strive for in our lives every day—freedom from whatever holds us back from achieving our true potential. Perhaps it's ego, laziness, or social pressure. Whatever it is, we should identify it and plan to extricate it from our lives so that we can grow to be the people we know we can be.

Rosh Hashanah is a celebration in marked contrast to the western view of a new year. For us it is a time of reexamination, when we recognize what is right and strive to return to that path. When the *shofar* blows, it is to awaken us out of our "sleep," that state of unconsciousness that allows us to slide into bad habits and poor judgments.

The Jewish year is more than a cycle, in which the same days keep coming around again ("Is it Passover already?"). It is a spiral. Yes, the day comes around again, but it has elevated us to a whole new level. From Passover to Passover, Rosh Hashanah to Rosh Hashanah, we should think about how we have grown.

Take the time to learn the significance and message of each holiday. Each one presents an opportunity to tap into the power of self-growth that God weaves into its essence. Each is a gift from your Creator. Use it well.

THE HOLIDAYS OF THE JEWISH YEAR

Passover

Time of year: Spring
Basis: Jews leaving Egypt
Concept/opportunity: Freedom of self
Tools: *Matzah*, Seder, *Haggadah*

Shavuot

Time of year: Early summer
Basis: Giving of the Torah
Concept/opportunity: Wisdom, direction, obligation
Tools: All-night Torah study

Tisha B'Av

Time of year: Summer
Basis: Destruction of both Temples and other tragedies
Concept/opportunity: Recognition of essential life values
Tools: Mourning and fasting

Rosh Hashanah

Time of year: Fall
Basis: Creation of mankind
Concept/opportunity: Self-evaluation; judgment
Tools: *Shofar*, prayer

Yom Kippur

Time of year: Fall
Basis: Forgiveness
Concept/opportunity: Return to true self
Tools: Teshuvah, fasting and prayer

Sukkot

Time of year: Fall
Basis: Jews traveling in the desert
Concept/opportunity: True security and happiness
Tools: *Sukkah*, *lulav* and *etrog*

Shemini Atzeret/Simchat Torah

Time of year: Fall
Basis: Jews traveling in the desert, physical preservation
Concept/opportunity: Love of Torah, Chosen People
Tools: Dancing, finishing reading the Torah and starting over

Chanukah

Time of year: Winter
Basis: Jewish revolt against the Greeks
Concept/opportunity: Courage to be Jewish
Tools: Lighting the *menorah*

Purim

Time of year: Winter/spring
Basis: Jewish people saved from Haman and the Persians
Concept/opportunity: Body/soul, joy
Tools: *Megillah* reading, sending gifts, helping the poor

In addition, modern holidays, such as Holocaust Memorial Day, Israel Independence Day, and Jerusalem Day, commemorate more recent historic events of importance to the Jewish people.

For Further Reading

Eliyahu Kitov, Nathan Bulman, translator, *The Book of Our Heritage* (New York: Feldheim Publishers, 1978); Shimon Apisdorf, *Judaism in a Nutshell: Holidays* (Baltimore: Leviathan Press, 2001); *Judaism in a Nutshell: Passover* (2001); *Chanukah: Eight Nights of Light, Eight Gifts for the Soul* (1997); *Survival Kit Family Haggadah* (1997); *One Hour Purim Primer* (1998); *Rosh Hashanah Yom Kippur Survival Kit* (1997); Rabbi Pinchas Stolper, *Living Beyond Time* (New York: Shaar Press, 2003); Ari D. Kahn, *Emanations* (Jerusalem: Targum Press, 2002).

✄ *Diary of Rememberance* ✄

Record here memories of spending holidays together. What special contribution did your loved one make to holiday celebrations?

_____

_____

_____

_____

_____

_____

_____

_____

_____

_____

_____

Our Merciful God in Heaven—May this portion of Torah learning be a merit and a blessing for my [relationship], [name]. May [his/her] soul be bound in the bond of life. May [his/her] resting place be that of peace.

Keeping Kosher

May God remember my [relationship], [name], *in whose merit I am now studying about my heritage of Judaism and the Torah.*

The Torah records 613 commandments (*mitzvot*). They fall into three categories:

1. *Mishpatim*: These are ordinances that a just society will naturally develop on its own. The reasons behind them are obvious and unquestionable. Examples are commandments like "Don't murder" and "Don't steal."
2. *Ediot*: These are laws of bearing witness. Examples are Kiddush (witness to creation), hearing the *shofar* blown (recognizing God as King), eating *matzah* (remembering God's love in bringing us out of Egypt), and so on.
3. *Chukim*: These laws don't have obvious explanations. Examples include separating milk and meat.

Why wasn't the Torah written in a way that listed each commandment with the reason for obeying it? Why give us some laws that have no explanation? One answer is that human nature uses the reason given for a rule as an excuse not to obey it.[52] For example, if your small child asks you if he can cut with a knife and you say no, he will counter with "Why not?"

And of course you will answer, "Because it's dangerous. You might hurt yourself."

Five minutes later you see your child using a knife. "What are you doing? I said you couldn't use a knife!"

Your child looks at you innocently. "I didn't hurt myself."

The Torah instructs us, "Do not boil a kid in its mother's milk." We learn not to combine milk with meat, but no explanation is given as to why.

Some people think that this line in the Torah is to teach us to be compassionate. How terrible, to boil a kid in its own mother's milk! That could very well be one of the reasons, but we can't then say we'll work on being compassionate and in the meantime eat cheeseburgers.

God understands that we are like this, trying to circumvent the letter of the law while upholding its spirit. So he gave us the Chukim with no explanation, and we are to fulfill them because we trust Him. He is saying that this commandment is so important He will not give us a reason that we can try to rationalize away. Do it, He says, because I say so. Do it because you trust Me.

But this isn't blind trust or a leap of faith. This trust is based on knowledge. This God who is telling us to separate milk and meat, a rule we don't clearly understand, is the same God who gave us commandments like "Don't steal," "Don't murder," "Don't commit adultery," and "Love your neighbor like yourself." These are laws that changed humanity for all time. They work. We can see that.

God, Creator of Heaven and earth, tells us not to murder, steal, or be sexually immoral and tells us to love one another, honor our parents, and set up courts of justice. We say, "Great!" So when He tells us not to cook milk and meat together, we should at least give it a chance, question it, investigate it, learn about it, and maybe try it out.

Although no reason is given for the commandment in the Torah and we fulfill it because we trust in God, knowing that He knows what is best for us, we are still responsible for analyzing the deeper messages behind it.[53]

Many great commentators have offered explanations. One is that since milk represents life and meat represents death, they just don't mix. We can also see a reason for the commandment by looking at some of the animals that we are forbidden to eat. For example, we are not allowed to eat birds of prey. What kind of life does an eagle or a falcon have? Unlike a chicken, it spends almost every waking moment killing in order to survive. By ingesting this bird whose whole drive is to kill, perhaps we somehow absorb that spirit.

People tell me that keeping kosher makes them feel very Jewish. Yom Kippur is once a year, and Shabbat is once a week. But we have to eat every day.

Keeping kosher also gives us a healthy feeling of setting physical limits. We can't simply eat anything we want. That control over our physical being helps us to grow spiritually.

When we don't completely understand the medicine prescribed, we trust that the doctor knows best and has our best interests at heart. So, too, with milk and meat. Keeping kosher is the original "soul food," and adhering to the laws has a great effect upon both body and soul. We may not completely understand it, but we know that God has in mind both our physical and spiritual good.

 For Further Reading

Rabbi S. Wagschal, *The New Practical Guide to Kashruth* (New York: The Judaica Press, 2003); Shimon Apisdorf, *Kosher for the Clueless but Curious* (Baltimore: Leviathan Press, 2005); Rabbi Eliezer Eidlitz, *Is It Kosher? An Encyclopedia of Kosher Food, Facts, and Fallacies* (New York: Feldheim, 1992); Susie Fishbein, *Kosher by Design* (New York: Artscroll, 2003).

Our Merciful God in Heaven—May this portion of Torah learning be a merit and a blessing for my [relationship], [name]. May [his/her] soul be bound in the bond of life. May [his/her] resting place be that of peace.

Friendship

May God remember my [relationship], [name], *in whose merit I am now studying about my heritage of Judaism and the Torah.*

Love your neighbor like yourself. I am God. (Leviticus 19:18)

We have all heard the famous statement, "Love your neighbor like yourself." But less known is what follows it: "I am God." Why are the two statements connected?

A story is told of a kingdom many years ago.[54] A terrible crime was committed within its walls and a man was accused, arrested, and sent to prison as it seemed he was the one guilty of the offense. The king decreed that he would die, but the man steadfastly professed innocence and demanded to see the king to plead on his own behalf. The king agreed, and the man came before him.

"I am innocent," he said, "and I have evidence to prove it."

"Show me your evidence," said the king.

The man explained that he could not, for the evidence was in another town and it would take days of travel to retrieve it. Only he knew how to get it and return it to the king.

"Do you think I'm just going to let you walk out of here on your word?" said the king. "How do I know you'll return?"

Just then a man stepped forward and said, "I will stand in place of my friend."

Now the king was intrigued. "All right," he said. "But if he does not return by sundown three days hence, you will die in his place. Agreed?"

"Agreed," said the friend.

The journey of the accused, however, was fraught with peril. Having gathered the evidence, he was on his way home when suddenly bandits surrounded him. They beat him and took all of his belongings, including the vital evidence that would exonerate him. Distraught and badly shaken, he kept on his way, determined to return in time to save his friend's life.

As he staggered through the gates, he could see the sun setting on the horizon. Finally he made it to the main square of the city minutes after sunset and with horror watched as his friend was led to the gallows.

Screaming with all his might, he yelled, "Stop! Stop the proceedings!" The execution was halted and the king was summoned.

The man explained to the king that he was unable to bring the evidence in time and demanded that his friend be released. He insisted that he should face whatever was his fate. But his friend, standing with hands shackled just steps from the gallows, refused to switch positions.

"The agreement stands," said his friend. "It is after sunset, and I am to die. You were required to be back by sunset."

"What are you talking about?" pleaded the man. "I'm back. I was the one convicted of the crime. You are completely innocent!"

"And so are you," answered the friend.

Back and forth the two friends went, each one arguing why the other should not die. Finally the king raised his hand for silence and spoke.

"I, the king of this land, hereby set you both free but under one condition: that you make me the third friend."

This story of friendship illustrates why the commandment to "Love your neighbor" appears with the words "I am God" immediately following it.

For the king in this story is the Almighty. When two people love each other, God says, "I want in on this. Let Me be part of this bond."

In our own lives, when we reach out and give to another with unselfish love, not only are we creating a relationship of tremendous strength and support, we are also inviting God to be part of it. And with Him, the possibilities of what we can achieve together are endless.

In times of need, we realize who our true friends are—not just acquaintances, but loyal, dedicated friends. In times of sorrow, those who love us come to listen, support, and care. We feel the incredible power of these friendships because when we create such a relationship, we bring God into the picture. Together, anything is possible.

For Further Reading

Rabbi Zelig Pliskin, *Love Your Neighbor* (New York: Aish HaTorah Publications); Rabbi Zelig Pliskin, *Harmony with Others* (New York: Artscroll-Mesorah, 2002); Rabbi Zelig Pliskin, *Kindness* (New York: Shaar Press, 2000).

❧ *Diary of Rememberance* ❧

How did your loved one look at friendship? Describe a special friendship that he or she had. Who was the friend? What did you learn by experiencing or observing the friendship?

_____

_____

_____

_____

_____

_____

_____

_____

_____

_____

Our Merciful God in Heaven—May this portion of Torah learning be a merit and a blessing for my [relationship], [name]. *May* [his/her] *soul be bound in the bond of life. May* [his/her] *resting place be that of peace.*

Teshuvah

*May God remember my [relationship], [name], in whose merit I
am now studying about my heritage of Judaism and the Torah.*

Everyone makes mistakes. The Torah is filled with people, great people, who made mistakes. Moses himself made mistakes. He was not allowed to enter the Land of Israel because of them. Our forefathers and foremothers were human, made of flesh and blood. Though they all achieved greatness, they also all made mistakes.

What does God want from us when we make mistakes? Teshuvah. The word teshuvah means "return." It is often mistranslated as "repentance." When we are asked by God to do teshuvah, we are asked by God to return.

If you are flying round-trip to Chicago, you leave your home and fly to Chicago. After you complete your stay, you use your return ticket to get on a plane and go back home. Returning means going back to somewhere you've been, somewhere familiar. When we do teshuvah, we return to the good person that we know we have been and can become again.

We all know when we stray, rationalize, bend the truth, avoid the effort, and ignore what is really important and meaningful in our lives. Mistakes come in all shapes and sizes. Often we know at the time that we shouldn't be doing what we are doing, but we are caught up, distracted, and convinced that somehow at the moment it is right.

God understands that. No one who has children expects them to be perfect. You know that as they grow they will make mistakes. Even when you tell them not to do something that will harm them, they do it anyway.

How do you want your children to feel when they err? Weighed down by guilt for life? Terrible about themselves? Of course not. You want them to recognize that they have made a mistake, to stop making it, to make it good, to learn from it, and to go on. Guilt is not a Jewish idea because guilt is paralyzing and self-absorbing. The Jewish view is to use mistakes to grow forward.

God is our Father in Heaven. He doesn't want us to be weighed down by negativity and self-loathing when we make mistakes. When we make the wrong choices in life, they should be seen as opportunities for growth, not chains and shackles to weigh us down forever.

Maimonides set out the steps for teshuvah.[55] When we make a mistake, we are to go through the process step by step. The result is forgiveness and growth.

- **Step 1: Stop.** Stop making the mistake. If you are losing your temper with others, stop.
- **Step 2: Regret.** You should indeed feel regret for your error. It's wrong to lose your temper, especially with someone that you love.
- **Step 3: Verbalize your regret.** Say it out loud to God. This doesn't have to be done at synagogue, it doesn't have to be only on Yom Kippur, and it doesn't have to be in Hebrew. Talk to God. Speak at least in an audible whisper (not only in your head). Tell Him that you are sorry and that you were wrong to lose your temper.

  If the mistake harmed other people (as opposed to a mistake between you and God, like eating something that wasn't kosher), then you have to make amends with that other person. After losing your temper, you must go to your friend and ask forgiveness.
- **Step 4: Make a plan.** How can you be sure that the mistake won't happen again? Make a practical plan of action. If you know that certain subjects are sources of conflict between you and your friend, perhaps make a pact to avoid those subjects for the sake of peace.

Once you have completed these steps for teshuvah, God accepts your return, and in the videotape of your life, those mistakes are edited out. At Rosh Hashanah and Yom Kippur, when God reviews your year of thoughts and deeds, He simply doesn't see those mistakes.

The completion of these steps is called *teshuvah gamurah*, or "complete return."[56] It occurs when God puts you in the same position as when you originally made the mistake and you do not repeat the mistake. In our example with your temper, it would be sometime later, perhaps sitting at a party with your friend, when someone brings up a touchy subject. If you hold your tongue and do not let yourself be pulled into an argument, you will have achieved *teshuvah gamurah*.

It is out of God's love for us that he gives us such a method of getting back on track. Put the guilt, shame, embarrassment, and negativity behind you. Let them go, and return.

For Further Reading

Shimon Apisdorf, *Rosh Hashanah Yom Kippur Survival Kit*, Chapter on *Teshuvah*: "Four Steps to Greatness" (Baltimore: Leviathan Press, 1994); Rabbi Pinchas Winston, *Changes That Last Forever* (New York: Feldheim, 1997); Adin Steinsaltz, *Teshuvah: A Guide for the Newly Observant Jew* (Lanham: Jason Aronson, 1996).

Diary of Rememberance

Was there conflict in your relationship with your loved one? Even though he or she is gone from this world, you can still make it right. Record here your feelings, and resolve to put the conflict behind you by going through the four steps of teshuvah.

_____

_____

_____

_____

_____

_____

_____

_____

_____

_____

_____

_____

Our Merciful God in Heaven—May this portion of Torah learning be a merit and a blessing for my [relationship], [name]. May [his/her] soul be bound in the bond of life. May [his/her] resting place be that of peace.

Love

May God remember my [relationship], [name], in whose merit I am now studying about my heritage of Judaism and the Torah.

Turn on the radio to any music station and you will undoubtedly hear the word "love" over and over again. Love is described as the key to everlasting happiness, the emotion that binds man to woman and woman to man. People spend a lifetime seeking it, sometimes with success and sometimes not. Some cross oceans to acquire it, write sonnets to glorify it, and even kill in its name. Such an important word! But if you ask a hundred people to define it, you may get a hundred different definitions.

In Judaism we say you must define your terms. Happiness, wisdom, and love are vitally important to us all. We want them, and yet we often fail to objectively discover their true meaning. It is much easier to find something once we really know what we're looking for.

If love is the basis for a happy marriage, what is the basis for love? Is it that state that we "fall" into? If so, we could just as easily fall out. Could love be so fleeting?

The Torah tells us that love is the emotion one feels when appreciating the virtues of another.[57] When looking for a marriage partner or when trying to build your marriage, ask yourself, "What do I appreciate about this person?" The more you choose to focus on the good qualities of your partner, the more love you will feel.

Our tradition teaches us that love is based on understanding. The more one knows about a person, the deeper the love. This knowledge creates a bond that grows with the marriage, not a fleeting feeling that may disappear at the first sign of conflict or unrest.

We have all heard the saying that "Love is blind," but this is not the Jewish view. Infatuation is blind. Love has both eyes open—we see the good, we see the bad, and we make a conscious choice to focus on the good.

The search for the perfect person is futile. You don't need a perfect person; you need a person perfect for you. And that means that he or she may have qualities that bother you. The Jewish view is that through marriage we will realize our potential. Doing so is not always easy. The qualities we dislike about our spouses may be the keys to helping us grow. Sometimes working on patience and forgiveness can develop the building blocks of self-actualization.

A rabbi told me the story of a man who kept a diary in which he tried to record one new virtue of his wife every day. This served many purposes. It gave him a reason to consciously look for the goodness in her and at the same time it served as a reminder during times of marital stress of just how much he loved her.

We have defined love, but what about marriage? In Judaism we say that an important part of marriage is the pursuit of mutual, meaningful life goals. Marriage is not just two people who happen to live in the same house and have children together.

What kind of goals are we talking about? Goals that answer the questions, What am I living for? What values do I want to give to my children? What kind of environment do I want to create in my home? What do I want to contribute to my community? What difference can I make to the Jewish people?

We may pursue and fulfill the goals in different ways, but we must be headed in the same direction. The more time and effort that we put into achieving these mutual goals, the more soundly we will build our marriages.

In our lives, we must see that love is not the unexplainable feeling described in song. It is the direct result of our choice to focus on the best in another person. This, along with the constant pursuit of mutual, meaningful life goals, can build a strong foundation that allows both partners to grow and achieve together.

 For Further Reading

Nachum Braverman and Shimon Apisdorf, *The Death of Cupid: Reclaiming the Wisdom of Love, Dating, Romance and Marriage* (Baltimore: Leviathan Press, 1997); R. Aharon Feldheim, *The River, the Kettle, and the Bird* (New York: Feldheim Publishers, 1987); Rabbi Pinchas Stolper, *The Sacred Trust* (New York: Artscroll, 1999); Gila Manolson, *Head to Heart* (New York: Targum Press, 2002); Manis Friedman, *Doesn't Anyone Blush Anymore?* (Brooklyn: Kehot, 1996); Esther Jungreis, *The Committed Marriage* (New York: HarperCollins, 2004).

Diary of Rememberance

You loved the person who passed away. What did you love about him or her? What did he or she teach you about love? Can you remember a story that illustrates one of your loved one's special virtues? Record it here.

_____

_____

_____

_____

_____

_____

_____

_____

_____

_____

_____

_____

Our Merciful God in Heaven—May this portion of Torah learning be a merit and a blessing for my [relationship], [name]. May [his/her] soul be bound in the bond of life. May [his/her] resting place be that of peace.

Day Twenty-two

Gratitude

May God remember my [relationship], [name], *in whose merit I am now studying about my heritage of Judaism and the Torah.*

From the day that God created the world, there was no one who thanked God until Leah came and thanked Him. (The Talmud[58])

Leah, married to Jacob, was one of the mothers of the Jewish people. In the passage above, the Talmud is referring to the birth of Leah's fourth son, Yehudah. The name Yehudah is derived from the word *thankfulness*, as in *todah*, the Hebrew word for "thank you." But what does the Talmud mean when it says that Leah was the first person to ever really thank God?

Abraham never thanked God? Noah never thanked God? Sarah never thanked God? Actually, they did. In fact, many people in the Torah had thanked God long before Leah. Therefore, the Talmud must be telling us that something was special about Leah's thankfulness. Her gratitude must have been somehow truer and deeper than that of anyone who had come before her. By understanding what made Leah's gratitude special, we will learn what true gratefulness is all about.

Leah was a prophetess who knew that the Jewish nation was destined to be formed from the twelve sons of Jacob, her husband. Each tribe would be a foundation stone that would shape our history. Jacob's sons would come from four women: Leah, Rachel, Bilha, and Zilpah. Leah expected that each woman would have three sons.

Yehudah was Leah's fourth son. She recognized that he was one more than her share. Her thankfulness for Yehudah was deeper and more heartfelt because he was unexpected. He was a gift.[59]

This is how we are supposed to view everything in life. Every ray of sunshine, every child, every breath—they are all gifts from God.

The mistake of thinking that anything is owed to us blocks us from gratitude.

People sometimes don't appreciate sight until they meet someone who is blind. We shouldn't wait until we are sick to appreciate our health. We should count our blessings every day and take pleasure in the miraculous gifts bestowed on us.

Jewish consciousness says that every morning we should rise with the prayer *"Modeh ani . . ."*: I thank God for bringing life to me each and every day.

At our time of sorrow, when we have lost a loved one, we are forced to stand and face our own mortality. We do not live forever, and we do not know from one day to the next when our time will come. All we can do is say, *"Modeh ani . . ."*: Thank you, God, for giving me another day and another opportunity to use it wisely.

Our religion is called "Judaism" from Judah, Yehudah. The essence of being a Jew is to be thankful. Realize, as Leah did, that every moment of life is a gift. Open the gift and take pleasure in its Source.

❧ *Diary of Rememberance* ❧

In what ways did your loved one express gratitude in his or her life?

_____

_____

_____

_____

_____

_____

_____

_____

_____

_____

Our Merciful God in Heaven—May this portion of Torah learning be a merit and a blessing for my [relationship], [name]. May [his/her] soul be bound in the bond of life. May [his/her] resting place be that of peace.

Abraham

May God remember my [relationship], [name], *in whose merit I am now studying about my heritage of Judaism and the Torah.*

Jewish tradition says that Abraham, the father of the Jewish people, was the epitome of greatness, and from him we learn vital lessons to help us as we live our own lives. Let us examine why.

God said to Abraham, go away from your land, and your birthplace, and from your father's house, to the land that I will show you. (Genesis 12:1)

This command is puzzling. At this point in the Torah, Abraham has already left his land and his birthplace. Why is God instructing him to leave a place that he has already left? The answer lies in understanding that Abraham's move is more than physical. God is asking him to make a journey not just of the body but of the soul.

The deeper meaning of leaving is reevaluating. God is asking Abraham to rethink his values and his goals and decide whether they are in fact his or simply the result of the environment in which he happened to be born.

Think for a moment about when and where you were born and raised. Under different circumstances, you could just as easily have been born in Switzerland or Poland or Africa. And here you are today. What if today were 1960 or 2160?

In a different place or time, we would probably be very different people with very different values. So would our children. What would stay constant? What are the values that shape our direction and establish our goals? These values go beyond the country listed on our passport or the era that we are born into.

A young person in the 1960s encountered philosophies of immense freedom and self-expression. Today the world has swung back to being more conservative and structured. Judaism says that trends are just that—they come and they go. Our challenge is to take the time to objectively reach beyond current fads and trends and embrace those critical values that affect us in a deeper, everlasting way.

When God asks Abraham to leave the land of his birth, he gives curious instructions. He says to go from your country, then from your city, then from your family's home. Normally when leaving, the order is reversed. You leave your home, then your city, and then your country.

This tells us that reexamining our values is easiest when we begin with the values of our country, for our country has the least impact compared to our community and, especially, our home. The order is not geographical but personal.

What we believe in, what we stand for, and what we are living for should be well thought out, not dependent on where we happen to reside or what is in fashion. This thought process takes effort and sometimes a little pain.

The message of Abraham is that all of us must stop and think, What do I really believe in? What are my goals in life?

The greatness of Abraham is that he heard this message from the Almighty and went forth on such a quest of self-discovery.

∽ Diary of Rememberance ∾

What did your loved one teach you about life's values? Was it taught by words or by example?

_____

_____

_____

_____

_____

_____

_____

_____

_____

_____

Our Merciful God in Heaven—May this portion of Torah learning be a merit and a blessing for my [relationship], [name]. May [his/her] soul be bound in the bond of life. May [his/her] resting place be that of peace.

Day Twenty-four

Who Is Wise?

May God remember my [relationship], [name], in whose merit I am now studying about my heritage of Judaism and the Torah.

Our sages teach that the key to wisdom is humility and the one thing that blocks our potential for wisdom is arrogance.[60]

If I told you that I would introduce you to the humblest man on earth, how would you picture him? You would probably imagine him as small, bent over, soft-spoken. Yet the Torah describes Moses as the humblest man who ever lived.[61] Moses, who stood up to Pharaoh in Egypt, secured the release of the Jewish people, scaled Mount Sinai, spoke to God face to face, led the Jews through the desert and to the Land of Israel.

How could a man who obviously possessed extraordinary qualities of leadership and strength be described as the humblest man who ever lived? Because humility is recognizing that we have tremendous skills, talents, and accomplishments but knowing that they are all from God. The humble person is not the lowly, hunched-over one—it is the person in touch with his or her greatness who knows that the greatness has a Source.

But aren't my accomplishments my own? Wasn't I the one who worked hard in school and in business?

A story is told of a man who receives an unexpected gift from his uncle. Later he tells the story, bursting with pride:

I was looking through the mail and I noticed a letter from my uncle. I had to open up the envelope and take out the letter that contained a check. I had to stand up and find my wallet. I had to open my wallet and put the check inside. Then I had to find a bank. When I got there, I had to open the door. Then I had to find the right line, stand there and follow the line to the teller. Then I had to lift the pen and sign my name. At last I had to take the money and put it in my wallet!

What's so difficult about cashing the check? we wonder. Who wouldn't cash it?

In life, you went to school. You worked hard. You found a job. We say that all of these accomplishments are great, but don't forget—you're just cashing the check. Who wrote it? God.

Don't take pride in accomplishments, take pleasure.

We all know that God is behind the scenes and is the source for all, but sometimes we forget.

A man comes over from Europe with five dollars in his pocket. After perseverance and hard work, he stands beside his successful factory and boasts, "Look what I built from nothing. I came here with five dollars in my pocket, and look what I made!" That night his factory burns down. The man rushes to the scene, looks up to the heavens and shakes his fist. "God, how could you do this to me?"

We make the mistake of thinking that on the way up it is we who build the success. But when things go wrong, we blame God. That is arrogance.

Humility is power because it means knowing that I don't have all the power, that some things are more important than me. When we rely only on ourselves, we are limited. But when we tap into the Source of it all, we are tapping into unlimited resources, unlimited potential, unlimited power. Now we can do anything.

Humility comes when you know what's important in life. One way to discover what that is to think, What would I sacrifice my life for? Would you sacrifice for your family? Your country? Your people? In Judaism we say, "When you know what you're willing to die for, then you know what to live for."[62] Many of us would give our lives for our families, and yet we spend little time with them compared to the time we spend at our businesses and at other activities. Some people in a time of danger would be willing to give their lives for the Jewish people or the Land of Israel, and yet today their time and resources are barely allocated to either one.

Our sages ask, "Who is wise?" They answer, "The one who learns from every person."[63] Does this mean a wise person has a lot of knowledge? To find out, let's look at Seder Night, at the Four Sons, and at the questions they ask from the *Haggadah*. The wise son asks, "What are these statutes and ordinances . . . ?"

Why is he called wise? It sounds as if he doesn't know anything. We call him wise because he is actively seeking to learn. He is curious, wants to grow, and values understanding.

Wisdom in Judaism does not belong to the person who has memorized the most of the Torah. Wisdom belongs to people who through humility are open to learning from every person they meet. Everyone has unique talents, skills, and life experiences that you can benefit from. When God sends someone your way, find out how you can learn from him or her and you too will be on the road to wisdom.

For Further Reading

R. Irving M. Bunim, *Ethics From Sinai* (New York: Feldheim Publishers, 1964); Rabbi Abraham J. Twerski, *Visions of the Fathers* (New York: Shaar Press, 1999); Rabbi Berel Wein, *Pirkei Avos: Teachings for Our Times* (New York: Shaar Press, 2003).

❧ *Diary of Rememberance* ❧

What important piece of life wisdom did your loved one give to you? Was it taught by words or by example?

_____

_____

_____

_____

_____

_____

_____

_____

_____

_____

Our Merciful God in Heaven—May this portion of Torah learning be a merit and a blessing for my [relationship], [name]. *May* [his/her] *soul be bound in the bond of life. May* [his/her] *resting place be that of peace.*

Day Twenty-five

Who Is Brave?

May God remember my [relationship], [name], *in whose merit I am now studying about my heritage of Judaism and the Torah.*

When we think of examples of bravery, we think of people like the racecar driver who travels at 160 miles per hour or the mountain climber who scales Mount Everest or the skydiver who jumps out of a plane.

But our sages don't cite such feats when discussing bravery. Our sages ask, "Who is brave?" The answer, "The one who conquers his *yetzer harah* (Evil Inclination)."[64] What is this Evil Inclination? Is it a little devil with a pitchfork perched on one shoulder while an angel, in opposition, sits on the other? Not exactly.

Within all of us exists an inner dialogue not between good and evil but between body and soul. The soul is connected to God and wants to do what is right, while the body wants to do what is easy. To live for what our souls want takes effort. The one who stands up and makes that effort exemplifies true bravery.

Abraham, our forefather, had many tests in his life, and our sages say that each one was more difficult than the last. At one point, the evil king Nimrod threw Abraham into a fiery furnace because of Abraham's beliefs (with divine intervention he survived). Later, God told Abraham to leave his home and go to another land (the Land of Israel).

But if the tests were progressively harder, that means that moving to an unknown land was more difficult than risking death in a fiery furnace. With Nimrod, Abraham was willing to make that one ultimate gesture and give his life for God. That was one level of pure sacrifice and commitment. But leaving his homeland to go to another land was an even greater level. Because greater than giving one's life for God is living each day for God.

Real bravery is getting up each day and making the effort to do what is right. That means standing up and fighting against what is holding us back in life, what is preventing us from realizing our true potential.

Pinpointing that enemy, making the effort, and ultimately being victorious calls on your personal courage. Your soul wants to get out of bed and accomplish great things with the day; your body wants to sleep. Your soul wants to take time for learning and wisdom; your body wants to tune out and watch TV. Your soul wants commitment and responsibility; your body wants to run away.

Your true essence is your soul. Harness the unlimited energy it possesses and you will come to know what courage is all about.

Our Merciful God in Heaven—May this portion of Torah learning be a merit and a blessing for my [relationship], [name]. *May* [his/her] *soul be bound in the bond of life. May* [his/her] *resting place be that of peace.*

Day Twenty-six

Who Is Rich?

May God remember my [relationship], [name], *in whose merit I am now studying about my heritage of Judaism and the Torah.*

Our sages ask, "Who is rich?" They answer, "The one who takes pleasure in what he has."[65]

We all know of very wealthy people who are terribly unhappy and quite ordinary people who are very happy. Happiness is the art of taking pleasure in what you have. Unhappiness is the art of focusing on what you don't have.

It's a glorious summer day. All your friends and family decide to go on a picnic. You pack a delicious lunch and travel to a picture perfect spot by a lake. The children frolic and play together. Adults stroll by the waterfront, breathing in the fresh air. Birds sing, and a soft breeze lovingly complements the warm sunshine. An occasional cloud drifts by, a small island in the deep blue sky.

You unpack the wicker-basket lunch of homemade breads, salads, meats, fruits, and drinks. The picnic table is spread with a red and white gingham cloth. Matching napkins adorn every plate.

But wait—something is missing! You frantically search the lunch basket, turning it over, shaking it furiously. "The mustard! We forgot to pack the mustard!" You collapse, devastated. The picnic is ruined. Who can enjoy a picnic of meats without mustard? You pack up and head for home.

Crazy? Of course! But this is what we do every day. Each morning we wake up, God has given us back our souls. We can breath, think, move, feel. We are sheltered, and we have food. We have family, and we have friends. And yet we spend a lot of our time worrying, being anxious, and complaining—about the weather, about the person in front of us who's driving too slowly, about the noisy neighbors, about a local politician, about five extra pounds, about the lousy paint job—about the mustard.

We are all looking for the mustard. Instead of counting our blessings and appreciating all that we have, we are continually focusing on what we don't have.

If someone offered you five million dollars for one of your eyes, what would you say? Forget it! But think for a moment. If you wouldn't give up one eye for five million dollars, that means you are walking around every day with at least ten million dollars.

We all have our "I would be happy if . . ." stories. I would be happy if I met the right person, bought that house, got that job, won that lottery.

But God wants us to be happy now. We are to take pleasure in all that we have, whether it is a lot or a little. If you are not happy with your portion in life, then it doesn't matter how much is in your bank account. It will never be enough. You can be a miserable millionaire.

Don't let your desire for the mustard blind you to the beauty and richness all around you, every moment, every day.

For Further Reading

Rabbi Zelig Pliskin, *Gateway to Happiness* (New York: Aish HaTorah Publications, 1983); Rabbi Zelig Pliskin, *Happiness* (New York: Artscroll-Mesorah, 1999); Rabbi Shmuel Dov Eisenblatt, *The Straight Way to Happiness* (New York: Feldheim, 2002); Alexander Aryeh Mandlebaum, *Simcha- The Spark of Life* (New York: Feldheim, 1995); Roiza Weinreich, *In Joy* (New York: Artscroll-Mesorah, 1993); Esther Jungreis, *The Committed Life* (New York: HarperCollins, 1999).

ᴖ *Diary of Rememberance* ᴖ

What made your loved one happy? Can you think of a time and a story to illustrate this? What did that teach you about life?

_____

_____

_____

_____

_____

_____

_____

_____

_____

_____

_____

Our Merciful God in Heaven—May this portion of Torah learning be a merit and a blessing for my [relationship], [name]. May [his/her] soul be bound in the bond of life. May [his/her] resting place be that of peace.

Who Is Honored?

May God remember my [relationship], [name], *in whose merit I am now studying about my heritage of Judaism and the Torah.*

Our sages ask, "Who is honored? The one who gives honor to all."[66] In our society, whom do we honor? The basketball player who makes millions of dollars for putting a ball through a hoop. The rock singer. The movie star. We applaud them when they perform, and yet when they grow older they are often ignored. What happened to the honor? Because it was based on superficial and meaningless qualities, it disappeared.

Judaism teaches that honor is the realization that everyone is created in the image of God and thus deserves to be treated with importance. Honor values people for their essence, for what is precious. This applies even if they seem ordinary or, as in the following story, annoying.

The great rabbi of the Talmud, Rabbi Hillel, was known to be highly developed in character and to possess extraordinary patience. Two students made a wager that they could annoy him to the point where he would lose his composure. The goal was to make Rabbi Hillel angry.[67]

They plotted and planned and at last put their scheme into action. The time was late Friday afternoon when everyone was very busy with last-minute preparations for Shabbat. The first young man approached Hillel's house and pounded on the door.

When Hillel opened the door, the young man began to ask him a nonsensical question. Hillel listened patiently and answered him, "My son, I believe this is the answer to your question." And then he proceeded to answer the silly inquiry as best he could.

They wished each other "Good *Shabbos*," and the boy departed while Hillel went back to his preparations.

Two minutes later, the other student banged on the door. Hillel again opened the door.

The scenario was repeated: a crazy question and the patient reply from Hillel, "My son, I believe this is the answer to your question."

"Good *Shabbos*," they said and parted. Of course, two minutes later the first student was back. The students repeated the ridiculous scenario time and time again until Shabbat arrived, but they were never able to witness even a glimmer of impatience from Hillel.

The key to his incredible patience can be seen in how he addressed the students. Each time he began, "My son . . ." For Hillel looked at every Jew as if he or she were truly family, and he focused on what was special about each one. We never give up on our children, even when they make mistakes time and time again, and Hillel applied this same treatment to every person who came his way.

Our sages also ask, "Who is honored? The one who honors others."[68] The person who lives life seeing the virtue in others is looked upon with the same high regard. Another saying from the sages asks, "Who is honored? The one who runs from honor."[69]

A man once went to his rebbe distressed. "I don't understand, Rebbe. According to the sages, I should be honored. I am living my life running from honor, and yet no one honors me."

"That," the Rebbe answered, "is because while you are running, you are always looking over your shoulder."

Diary of Rememberance

What one special quality did your loved one possess that brought natural recognition from others?

_____

_____

_____

_____

_____

_____

_____

_____

_____

_____

Our Merciful God in Heaven—May this portion of Torah learning be a merit and a blessing for my [relationship], [name]. *May* [his/her] *soul be bound in the bond of life. May* [his/her] *resting place be that of peace.*

Day Twenty-eight

Honoring Parents

May God remember my [relationship], [name], *in whose merit I am now studying about my heritage of Judaism and the Torah.*

Honoring parents is said to be one of the hardest commandments in the Torah.[70] But what does it mean to give your parents honor? Does it mean to do everything they say? What if you disagree with them?

The goal of this mitzvah is to give parents pleasure and to serve them. We do not have to live life according to their dictates, but our lives and deeds should be a credit to them.[71]

We make the mistake of thinking that our parents owe us. We think, of course they should feed and clothe us, pay for our education and our weddings. After all, we didn't ask to be born, right? Wrong. Our parents don't owe us. We owe them. They gave us life.

The gratefulness that we should feel for this gift of life should inspire us to give back to our parents. Our gifts don't necessarily have to be material ones. The Talmud says that we can serve our parents elaborate food fit for a king and not fulfill the mitzvah of honoring them. Yet it goes on to say that we can serve them plain barley and show them great honor. The difference is in our attitude.[72]

What is our motivation when we are doing things for our parents? Physical and material gestures are futile if they are offered without the intent of showing gratitude for all that they have given us.

But what about all the things they did wrong? What if my parents were too critical or negative? Why should I be grateful?

Imagine it is your twentieth birthday. Your parents surprise you with a brand new car! You run out in excitement, but you stop in your tracks when you see it. It doesn't have wheels! You are furious and spend the next weeks sitting in the house pouting. After all, what good is a car without wheels? What should you do? Go out, earn some money, and buy the wheels.

In life, we are often too quick to blame our parents for our problems and shortcomings. But we are acting like the person who gets the car without the wheels. Did our parents make mistakes raising us? Of course they did! Everyone makes mistakes. Our challenge in life is to accept what they gave us—the good and the bad—and make our maximum effort in life. Our parents' mistakes do not eliminate our obligation to give them honor.[73] Again: they gave us life.

Even if we disagree with them, we must do it carefully. We should not contradict, correct, or shame them. We must refrain from talking harshly to them. If they say something wrong, instead of saying, "Dad, you're wrong," we should try, "Dad, it seems to me that . . ." Your motivation and attitude make the difference.

We learn something priceless when we fulfill this commandment. Showing gratitude to our parents teaches us how to be grateful to God.

The Ten Commandments that Moses brought down from Mount Sinai are listed on the tablets in an interesting way. On the right tablet are the commandments regarding the laws between a person and God ("Don't worship idols"), and on the left tablet the laws between people ("Don't murder"). Yet on the right with the commandments between a person and God is the mitzvah to honor one's parents.

We learn from this that the relationship between parents and children has very much to do with our relationship with God. Having children teaches us kindness because we give to them constantly and unselfishly. We also learn mercy because we forgive them even when they make the gravest mistakes (and even when we told them not to make the mistake). And we love them more than life itself.

God is always giving to us—every day, every flower, every raindrop, every breath. And He forgives us even when we make grave mistakes (even if He clearly told us not to make the mistake). And He loves us more than our parents loved us and more than we will ever love our children. The all-encompassing devotion we get from our parents and transmit to our children gives us just an inkling of what it means to have that same love from God.

That is why we must teach our children to honor us. It's not for us but for them. It is the only way they can develop that important relationship with their Creator, a bond that will carry them through all that life will bring.

Maimonides says that this commandment extends even after our parents are gone.[74] Remembering them through our learning, prayers, thoughts, and words is a continuation of honor.

This commandment for life extends beyond life itself. To strive as best we can to fulfill it properly means the deepest rewards here and for eternity.

For Further Reading

Moshe Lieber, *The Fifth Commandment: Honoring Parents* (New York: Artscroll-Mesorah, 1998).

❧ *Diary of Rememberance* ❧

What do you plan to do now and in the future to honor your parents?

_____

_____

_____

_____

_____

_____

_____

_____

_____

_____

_____

Our Merciful God in Heaven—May this portion of Torah learning be a merit and a blessing for my [relationship], [name]. May [his/her] soul be bound in the bond of life. May [his/her] resting place be that of peace.

Day Twenty-nine

Jerusalem

May God remember my [relationship], [name], in whose merit I am now studying about my heritage of Judaism and the Torah.

A story in our tradition goes as follows: [75]

Two brothers grew up on a farm on the side of a mountain. One brother married and moved to the other side of the mountain. Soon he had children, but he was never able to make his new land prosper. The brother who stayed to work the family farm prospered greatly with harvests in abundance, yet he remained alone and unmarried.

The unmarried brother sat up at night, unable to sleep knowing that his married brother was struggling to make ends meet. One night he decided to take some of his crops secretly to his brother's home. He did not want to embarrass him, so he put them on his brother's land quietly and went away.

On the other side of the mountain the other brother was also up every night because here he was happily married with children while his brother on the other side of the mountain was alone. What could he possibly do to comfort him? All he had to offer were some meager crops, so he bundled them up. In the middle of the night he traveled over the mountain and was able to sneak them onto his brother's land

Night after night the same scene occurred, each brother, unbeknown to the other, traveled over the mountain with his bundle of crops. The secret giving continued for weeks. But one star-filled night, it happened that one brother was traveling over the mountain at the same time as the other. They met at the top of the mountain, and each saw the other carrying a bundle of crops. The realization of what had been going on struck both of them at the same time. Overwhelmed with emotion, they dropped their bundles and embraced.

And God looked down and said, "On that spot will be Jerusalem."

Jerusalem. The very word brings forth so much feeling and longing. It is a word that literally means "the City of Peace." *Shalom* (peace) is also connected to the word *shalaym*, which means "complete." The story of the two brothers is a story of what it means to be a giver. And to be a giver is to be like God.

The book of Genesis tells us that Abraham our forefather was in his tent when God came to him. At that moment, three strangers approached from outside and Abraham ran out to greet them and offer them food and rest.[76]

The Talmud asks how it can be that Abraham would leave God's presence to do kindness for three strangers.[77] This is the answer given: "Greater than being in the presence of God is being like God."

Abraham embodied *chessed* (giving). He was emulating the Almighty, the ultimate giver. And our sages say that giving leads to loving. The more that we give to someone, the closer we will feel to them. The ultimate *shalom*, the ultimate peace, is to be whole, *shalaym*, complete. Giving leads to completion, while taking causes separation.

The creation of the world was an act of kindness, an act of giving. Our tradition points to Jerusalem as the world's center, its heart.

Doing what is right, giving to others, loving every Jew—this is where the body and soul meet. It is the integration of all that Jerusalem is—whole and complete, the eternal heart of the Jewish people. It is a living symbol of who we are and all that we strive for.

For Further Reading

Rabbi Aryeh Kaplan, *Jerusalem—Eye of the Universe* (New York: NCSY Publications, 1993).

Our Merciful God in Heaven—May this portion of Torah learning be a merit and a blessing for my [relationship], [name]. May [his/her] soul be bound in the bond of life. May [his/her] resting place be that of peace.

Day Thirty

Struggling With God

May God remember my [relationship], [name], *in whose merit I am now studying about my heritage of Judaism and the Torah.*

Sometimes we feel angry with God. Sometimes we feel He is very far away. Sometimes we feel that our relationship with Him is in conflict. Yes, sometimes we struggle with God. And that's okay.

We are called "B'nai Yisrael" (the Children of Israel.)[78] Yisrael means "to struggle with God." That is who we are. We are a people who struggle with our relationship with our Creator.

The first of the Ten Commandments begins, "I am God who took you out of the land of Egypt . . ." Maimonides states that this is the commandment "to know there is a God."[79] But how do we know anything? And how does this differ from having faith?

How do you know someone loves you? Think about it. Perhaps she tells you that she loves you; she shows you her love through her actions; you experience her love in a myriad of ways. You could produce concrete evidence that she loves you. You would not say, "I have faith that she loves me." You would relate all the stories and present all the evidence clearly attesting to her love.

Knowledge is active. It implies effort to understand and to gather evidence. It takes work to really know something. It is a process of questioning and, yes, struggle.

The exact middle word of the Torah is *darash*, which means "to inquire, to question."[80] The central word of our Torah is the central concept in our efforts to understand and come close to the Almighty.

Do not feel guilty if you feel angry with God. There is something that is much worse—not having a relationship with Him at all. Sometimes you may feel He is far away. He is not, but those feelings are a normal and sometimes necessary part of the relationship.

When we are struggling with our relationship with God, we are fulfilling the first of the Ten Commandments; we are making an effort to really know. This does not mean that we shouldn't trust in God. We should. However, our trust should be grounded in knowledge. Trusting in God does not mean giving up your mind; it means using it.

God gave you life: every raindrop, every heartbeat, every child's smile. They are all gifts. But these gifts are temporary. They are for this world, and they are for our pleasure, but they are limited. The greatest gift is what He placed inside of us all. It is the gift of the *neshama*, of the soul. God made each person unique not only on the outside (think—out of billions of people, no two are exactly alike) but on the inside as well.

And no matter how long a person lived in this world, who that person was, his or her essence, stays with us and lives on in another world for eternity. We remember our loved ones and we try to live our lives differently because we knew them here and because we want to make a difference for them there.

For Further Reading

Rabbi Aryeh Kaplan, *If You Were God* (New York: NCSY Publications); Rabbi Aryeh Kaplan, *The Infinite Light* (New York: OU-NCSY, 1993); Rabbi David Aaron, *The Secret Life of God* (Boston: Shambhala, 2004); Benjamin Blech, *If God is Good, Why Is the World So Bad?* (Deerfield Beach: Simcha Press, 2003); Shimon Apisdorf, *Judaism in a Nutshell: God* (Baltimore: Leviathan Press, 2001).

Our Merciful God in Heaven—May this portion of Torah learning be a merit and a blessing for my [relationship], [name]. *May* [his/her] *soul be bound in the bond of life. May* [his/her] *resting place be that of peace.*

Section Three:

A Guided Journey through Shiva and the Stages of Jewish Mourning

*J*udaism provides a beautiful, structured approach to mourning that involves three stages. When followed carefully, these stages guide mourners through their tragic loss and pain and gradually ease them back into the world. One mourner said her journey through the stages of mourning was like being in a cocoon. At first she felt numb and not perceptively alive, yet gradually she emerged as a butterfly ready again to fly.

The loss is forever, but the psychological, emotional, and spiritual healing that takes place at every stage is necessary and healthy. The system brilliantly addresses so many of the issues facing a person at this difficult time.[1]

STAGE ONE: SHIVA

Imagine you are driving in a Jewish neighborhood in any city in North America and your car breaks down. You have left your cell phone at home, and you have to call your spouse and/or the auto club. Across the street you see a house with a lot of people streaming in and out. You hear laughter, and the mood is festive. You figure that perhaps you could go in and ask to use a phone.

As you approach the house, you hear animated conversations about people's vacations, businesses, and lives. You walk in the door and see waiters, waitresses, and tables laden with food.

If you didn't know you were at a shiva, where would you think you were? At a party—perhaps someone's birthday, an anniversary, or some other *simcha* (joyous celebration). Festive events like these are what shivas have become, and they are a travesty of what a house of mourning is supposed to be.

The traditional shiva is very different. You walk into the house. No one greets you at the door or takes your coat. There is no laughter, no food, and no merriment. The mourners are sitting on short chairs, their clothes are torn, and they look awful. People are crying.

For the one paying the shiva call, this can be unnerving. Getting lost in a party is easier than facing real grief and mourning.

Everyone is somewhat aware that shiva parties are wrong. But no one knows how to turn the clock back and make them right. In this section you'll find many suggestions.

WHAT IS SHIVA?

After a burial, the direct mourners return to a home called the shiva house to begin a seven-day period of intense mourning. Shiva comes from the word *sheva*, which means "seven." What the mourners do this week is called "sitting shiva" and is an emotionally and spiritually healing time during which the mourners sit low and dwell together, and friends and loved ones come to comfort them with short visits referred to as "shiva calls."

LAWS OF MOURNING

The laws of mourning explained in this section address various aspects of grief; many have the purpose of focusing a person on his or her own spirituality. As you will see by the laws, we experience a feeling of physical discomfort as we totally focus on the soul of the one who has departed. We de-emphasize our own physicality by not pampering our bodies so we remember that what we are missing at this time is not the physical person who is gone but the essence of who that person was, which of course is the soul.

The overall focus throughout the week of shiva is this: I am a soul; my loved one is a soul.

SITTING SHIVA

People are confused about how to sit shiva and how to properly pay a shiva call. Because people do not know how and because talking about death makes people nervous and awkward, the shiva house often turns into a festive gathering filled with nervous chatter instead of the proper house of mourning.

Remember, our traditions and laws of death and mourning are not empty rituals handed down from our grandparents. The Torah itself speaks about the mourning of Aaron for his sons and Joseph for Jacob. Amos the prophet discusses mourning. It is considered a sacred observance dating back even before the giving of the Torah. The flood of Noah was postponed because the world was in mourning for Methuselah.[2] The Talmud speaks about the laws of mourning not because God wanted to fill our lives up with a lot of dos and don'ts but because if one properly mourns according to Jewish law and tradition, the important emotional, spiritual, and psychological healing will take place.

The pain of loss is great. But if properly conducted, the seven-day period of shiva can be the first step in dealing with this tremendous and tragic loss. Without it and without the other stages of mourning that we will discuss, the mourner may never be able to properly go on with life.

Who Sits Shiva? One sits shiva if one has lost a parent, spouse, sibling, or child. All other loved ones are also mourned, but the observances of shiva apply only to the direct mourner.

The Timing of Shiva. The seven-day period of mourning begins immediately after the burial. Thus, the first day of shiva is the day of the burial.

If the funeral was on a Tuesday, the last day of shiva is the following Monday. If a Jewish holiday (for example, Rosh Hashanah) falls during the seven days, the shiva continues until the holiday and then ends. In such a case, the mourner is considered to have mourned for the seven days even though the period was cut short.

If a person passes away during a holiday, the burial and shiva are conducted when the holiday is complete.[3] If a person passes away on Shabbat, the burial is performed the next day.

When Shabbat falls during the shiva, it is counted as one of the seven days of mourning, but one does not mourn publicly. This means that the outer signs of mourning (covering mirrors that others can see, sitting low, wearing no makeup, wearing mourner's garments, etc.[4]) are suspended because the joy of Shabbat overrides even public mourning. The outer signs of mourning are suspended before the beginning of Shabbat so that a person has time to properly prepare (shower, dress, and so on) for Shabbat. On Saturday night the shiva resumes. On Shabbat, people sitting shiva mourn in their hearts.

The Three-Day Shiva. Nothing in our tradition supports the concept of sitting shiva for three days. The number seven (*sheva*) in Judaism is very significant for it symbolizes completion in this world, as in the seven days of creation.

The current trend to sit for only three days comes from the mistaken belief that it will somehow make the mourning easier not to "drag it out." And if the shiva, because of a lack of knowledge, becomes a series of festive social gatherings, then who would want to socialize for seven days after experiencing a devastating loss?

Observed in the proper way, each one of the seven days is important. These are not easy days, for sitting shiva is emotionally and physically draining, but this time is crucial both for the mourner and for the soul that has passed on to the next world. Observing shiva gives honor to the loved one, and the merit of the observance is an elevation of the departed soul. If part of the family wants to sit for only three days, so be it. Just go to your home after their shiva ends and sit for the rest of the days in personal mourning. You don't have to make a public statement about it as you must be careful of their feelings.

I had an adult student who was told to sit shiva for her mother for three days. I wanted to convince her otherwise but felt uncomfortable about doing so at such a time. I paid a shiva call to her, and if I hadn't known someone had died, I would have thought I had walked into a cocktail party with a lot of food, laughter, and drinks. I finally found my student, who was directing the waitresses in the kitchen. I took her by the hand and sat her down and talked to her about her mother and about the soul and the afterlife. I told her that she didn't have to do this—all the food, drinks and entertaining. She said, "I know, but everyone expects me to." I mentioned that really the shiva should be seven days, but she answered, "Who would want to do this for seven days? I want everyone to leave me alone. My mother is dead!"

Weeks later she called me to tell me that even with the party atmosphere, sitting for only three days was a mistake. She said at the end of the three days people left, her husband went back to work, and everyone expected her to resume her life. "But," she cried to me, "I haven't mourned my mother."

After the Burial. Immediately upon returning from the cemetery after the burial and before entering the shiva house, the mourners and anyone else who attended the burial perform a ceremonial washing of the hands (using washing stations provided by the funeral home or buckets and a cup). When one has come in contact with death, it is proper to pour water three times over each hand (alternating hands each time) in order to focus on life. Why water? Water is the source of all life, and thus we pour it over our hands as a physical act that has spiritual ramifications.

The Focus. From the time of death until the conclusion of the funeral, the primary focus and concern is on the care of the deceased and the burial preparations. The care for the departed before burial, the eulogy, the actual burial—all are done to honor the one who has died, not to comfort the mourners.

However, once shiva begins, the focus shifts to the mourners. The mourners experience a week of intense grief and the community is there to love and comfort and provide for their needs. This is a critical point, for if one must feel the heart-wrenching pain of grief and loss, it should be done at a time when all those around are there to help and comfort.

Getting Up from Shiva. The seventh and final day of shiva is observed only for a few short hours, although this counts as a whole day.[5] After the last Shacharit (morning) service, the mourners sit low again for a short time. Then those who have come to comfort the mourners say to them, "Arise."[6] The comforters then say:

> No more will your sun set, nor your moon be darkened, for God will be an eternal light for you, and your days of mourning shall end. (Isaiah 60:20)

> Like a man whose mother consoles him, so shall I console you, and you shall be consoled in Jerusalem. (Isaiah 66:13)[7]

The mourners acknowledge that the shiva is over by leaving the shiva house publicly for the first time, taking a short walk around the block with those who have come to comfort them.

The house that the mourners live in for the week of shiva becomes a house of mourning. It takes on an ambience of solemnity, filled with memory, contemplation, and meditation. But it is a house where people will continue to dwell. The concrete act of physically stepping outside, walking around the block, and coming back in states that this house and the mourners' relationship with this house will now be renewed.

THE SHIVA HOUSE AND PROPER ARRANGEMENTS FOR SHIVA OBSERVANCE

This week of mourning is intensely private but shared with community, friends, and family. Ideally, all the direct mourners sit shiva in the house of the deceased for it says, "Where a man lived, there does his spirit continue to dwell."[8] Thus the presence of the person who has passed away is strongest in his or her own home. But one may sit shiva in any home. Any home of one of the direct mourners will be filled with the spirit of the loved one who is now gone. Memories will come easily there, and part of the comfort of the week of shiva is sharing such memories.

The best practice is for the mourners to move into the shiva house together for the week. If this is not possible, designate one home as the shiva house, and those who cannot sleep there may leave after dark to go home and return to the shiva house early in the morning.

Mourners should ideally not leave the shiva house at any time. Others must take care of any errands or outside commitments for them. To be seen during the day in public would force one to put on a public "face," which is inappropriate during this time. When family, friends, and neighbors help out during the week and provide for the needs of the mourners, an atmosphere of love, caring and kindness is created. This helps to soften the pain that the mourners so deeply feel.

The proper physical setup of the shiva house includes the following items:

Memorial Candle. A person's soul is compared to a flame since each person brings light into the world. And just as one can take from a flame to light more candles without diminishing the original flame, so too a person can give of himself or herself, touching many lives, without ever being diminished.

The wick and the flame are also compared to the body and soul and the strong bond between them. And just as a soul always strives upward for what is good and right, so too a flame can only burn toward the heavens.

Thus a memorial candle is lit in the shiva house and remains burning publicly twenty-four hours a day throughout the entire week. The funeral home usually provides these candles.

When you look at the candle, remember that your loved one's soul is eternal. This thought can help bring light into the darkness that you are now immersed in.

Chairs. Those mourners sitting shiva are required to sit low as a sign of mourning. Funeral homes often provide chairs with shortened legs for this purpose. One can also remove the cushions of a couch or chair and use that. Some have the custom of actually sitting on the floor. This is a physical symbol of the loneliness and depression a mourner feels.

Regular chairs should be placed in front of the mourner so those visitors paying a shiva call can sit close and provide emotional comfort. Setting up the shiva house in this way will help the visitor know the proper thing to do when calling upon the mourner (see "Paying a Shiva Call" later in this section).

Mirrors. Proper practice is to cover the mirrors in the shiva house (with sheets or fogged spray provided by the funeral home) for the following reasons:

- The mourners are striving this week to ignore their own physicality and vanity in order to concentrate on the reality of being a soul.
- Physical relations between a husband and wife are suspended during the week of shiva, and thus the need for physical beauty is removed.
- A mirror represents social acceptance through the enhancement of one's appearance. Jewish mourning is supposed to be lonely

and silent, with the mourner dwelling on his or her personal loss. Covering the mirrors symbolizes this withdrawal from society's gaze.

- Prayer services, commonly held in the shiva house, cannot take place in front of a mirror. When we pray, we focus on God and not on ourselves.

A Notice to Help Those Paying a Shiva Call. The Dans, a family that we are close to, lost their mother. Realizing that people, both Jewish and non-Jewish, coming to comfort them would not necessarily know what to do, Michael Dan composed this notice and posted it outside their front door. I thank him for allowing me to reprint it. A copy that you can use is offered at the end of the book.

In a Jewish House of Mourning

Each culture approaches death and the mourning period in its own unique fashion. As a family, we only request that an effort be made to create an atmosphere that is congruous with our Jewish values. Conversations should focus on the life and legacy of Judy Dan. No effort should be made to portray her in an artificial light, since this would offend her memory. Painful as it may seem, attempts at distracting family members from thinking or speaking about their loss are not considered appropriate at this time.

Thank you.
The Dan Family

Perhaps those in a similar situation could use Michael's words as a guide for composing their own notice. Visitors, upon reading such a message, will walk into the shiva home knowing what is proper to say and do. Such a message will help them and, by creating the proper atmosphere in the shiva home, will also help the mourners.

THE MOURNER

The Mourners' Meal. The first thing that the mourners do upon entering the shiva house is to sit down (again, low) to a "meal of condolence." This meal is supposed to be provided by neighbors or the community in order to show the mourners that those around them wish to provide consolation.

Another, deeper psychological reason lies behind this gesture for it recognizes that mourners, having just returned from the heavy trauma of the burial, may harbor a death wish for themselves and not want to go on living any more without their loved one. The meal they must eat speaks to that part of them and says, "No, you must go on. You must affirm life and live."

This first meal is eaten silently, and it includes the following foods:
- Bread—considered the sustenance of life
- Hard-boiled eggs—a food that is round, like the cycle of life
- Cooked vegetables and/or lentils—lentils again being round
- Coffee and tea

All other meals during the shiva should ideally be prepared or sent by others. The mourner always eats sitting low.

Kaddish and Prayer Services. Prayer services are held for the mourners and those present in the shiva house and not in the synagogue. One reason for this is to ensure that for the week of shiva the mourners do not have to leave the home where they are best able to fully experience the mourning process. They do not have to dress up to go out or to put on a public face for anyone. The services come to them.

It is certainly appropriate and poignant to have services in the home itself for the center of Jewish life is the home. This is the place where Jewish values are passed down. This is where family celebrations take place and where joys are shared. It is also where pain and loss are shared. It is where Judaism lives.

Traditional services are usually held in the morning (called Shacharit) and in the late afternoon/evening (called Mincha/Maariv). Between the Mincha and Maariv services, it is appropriate for someone to share some thoughts from the Torah in memory of the departed. It is good to pay a shiva call during these times if a quorum of people is needed to conduct the service. A *minyan*, traditionally ten men, is the minimum required for the mourners to say Kaddish.

During all of the services, the mourners recite the Kaddish.

Work. With some exceptions, a mourner refrains from going to work during the week of shiva. The rabbi should be consulted if pressing financial matters are at hand. Again, shiva is a deeply personal time of reflection, coming to terms with loss and grief, and contemplating the inner spiritual dimensions of life. The workplace draws our thoughts and feelings outward; thus, if at all possible, work should be avoided.

Shoes. A mourner should either be in stocking feet or wear slippers not made of leather. This symbolizes, again, the disregard for vanity and physical comfort.

What to Refrain From. One who is mourning should refrain from the following activities:
- Bathing or showering for pleasure (one may do it for cleanliness)
- Anointing (with creams, perfume, etc.)
- Wearing makeup
- Getting a haircut (this applies for the first thirty days)
- Trimming nails

- Wearing freshly laundered garments for pleasure (may be worn for cleanliness)
- Wearing new clothing
- Washing clothes
- Engaging in marital relations

PAYING A SHIVA CALL

The following ideas will help ensure that your visit to a mourner is appropriate, meaningful, and comforting.

The Focus. When one pays a shiva call, the focus is on comforting the mourners in the time of their greatest grief. Traditionally, one enters the shiva house quietly with a small knock so as not to startle those inside. No one should greet visitors; they simply enter on their own.

Food or drinks are not laid out for the visitors because the mourners are not hosts. They do not greet the visitors, rise for them, or see them out.

One who has come to comfort a mourner should not greet the mourners. In fact, the best practice is to come in silently and sit down close to them. Take your cue from them. If they feel like speaking, let them indicate it to you by speaking first. Then you can talk to them, but what about? Again, let them lead and talk about what they want to talk about. Speaking about the one who has passed away is best, and if you have any stories or memories to share with the mourner, this is the time to share them.

This is not a time to distract the bereaved from their mourning. Out of our nervousness, we often babble on about trivialities because we do not know what to say.

Often, the best thing to say is nothing.[9] A shiva call can sometimes be completely silent. If the mourners do not feel like talking at that time, so be it. Your goal is not to get them to talk; it is to comfort them. Your presence alone is doing that. By sitting there silently, you are saying more than words can. You are saying, "I am here for you. I feel your pain. There are no words."

And sometimes there aren't. Here are examples of things not to say:

"How are you?" What can the grieving person reply? No words can describe how a mourner feels.

"I know how you feel." Even if you yourself have experienced a loss, no one truly knows what another person is feeling. Don't pretend to. Each person feels a unique loss. Don't diminish a mourner's feelings with words that can never be true.

"At least she lived a long life." Someone who had lost her father told me that she hated it when people said that to her. She wanted to scream, "That means I loved him a long time, and his death is killing me!"

"It's good that you have other children," or, "Don't worry; you'll have more." It doesn't matter if you have 100 children. The loss of a child, no matter what age, is devastating.

"Cheer up—in a few months you'll meet someone new." This is not the time to think of remarriage. When people have lost a spouse, they have lost the other half of their soul. It is not appropriate during the shiva to speak of new relationships.

"Let's talk about happy things." Comforting a mourner does not mean distracting a mourner. Don't fill in the time talking about happy subjects or inconsequential topics like politics or business. Remember that speaking about the departed loved one is comforting. It's all right if mourners cry; they are grieving. This is all part of the important process of coming to grips with such a loss.

"It's all for the best." Losing a loved one never feels as if it is for the best.

"In time you will feel better." Even though this is true, the mourner does not want to hear it. No future exists at this point, only the present. And the present hurts.

By being silent and just being there for your friend or relative, or by sharing words and memories about the loved one, you will be comforting the mourner. If you didn't know the person who passed away (but are there because you have a relationship with one of the mourners), let the mourners tell you about their loved one if they feel so inclined. Sometimes it will be too painful. Again, take the lead from them.

When to Pay a Shiva Call. Do not make a shiva call on Shabbat or on a holiday, when no public mourning takes place.

Leaving a Shiva House. Even for a visit in silence, there is a traditional statement of comfort that you say to one who is mourning just before you leave the shiva house (it can be said in either Hebrew or English):

Ha-makom y'nachem etchem b'toch sh'aar aveilei tzion v'yirusholayim.

May God comfort you among the other mourners of Zion and Jerusalem.

God in this line is referred to as "Hamakom" (the Place). By saying this to the mourner, you are stating that He is everywhere, that we exist within Him here and in the next world. The person who is gone is still connected to you for you are together, contained within "the Place."

"Among the other mourners" speaks about the Jewish people. You are saying that we are family. Some people are close and some are distant cousins, but the loss of even one Jew makes us all mourners.

"Of Zion and Jerusalem" speaks of our collective mourning because of the destruction of the Temple in Jerusalem, the central point of the Jewish relationship to God that was destroyed by the Romans 2,000 years ago.[10]

The mourner should nod or say "Amen," and you should quietly depart, making sure that the mourner does not get up to see you out.

Paying a shiva call can be awkward at first. Keep in mind that you may have to modify it for those who are unaware of our traditions. If the mourner would think it odd that you would come in and not say anything, then of course you can speak and offer your condolences.

But at one shiva call I paid, to a person who is not completely observant, I came in, sat beside her, took her hand, and said nothing. She started to cry and said, "There are no words." I said, "I know." And let's face it, there aren't.

STAGE TWO: SHLOSHIM

The first thirty days following the burial (which include the shiva) are called the shloshim from the Hebrew word meaning "thirty".

Most restrictions that applied to mourners during the seven-day shiva period are now lifted. For the next twenty-three days, mourners are allowed to leave their house and begin to work again. However, they should severely limit social engagements during this time, and certainly avoid festive outings where music is played. Mourners do not shave or cut their hair during this time.

One is still mourning, but during the shloshim the laws allow for a gradual reentry into everyday life. For mourners to get up from the shiva and jump back into a normal routine would not be healthy. They are still mourning, even though the intense pain has now become almost bearable. Moments of deep sadness and longing are to be expected, and having these few restrictions reminds them, and reminds the people around them, that this is a process that certainly isn't over.

After the completion of the shloshim, if mourners are mourning anyone but a parent, the official mourning now ends. That means Kaddish is no longer recited and they can resume activities without restriction.

Why thirty days? The Jewish calendar is marked according to lunar time. As the moon waxes and wanes in a cycle, the thirty-day period of mourning is an opportunity for a person to emotionally come full circle. The process begins with the funeral and the first days of shiva, when not even a glimmer of light is seen. As time goes on, the light slowly comes back, fuller and fuller. The thirty days is an important central cycle of time, a time to renew oneself and to come to grips with a new reality.

Of course mourners still feel the pain of the loss, but Judaism recognizes that to a certain degree, the passage of time is able to ease and heal the pain. Being able to return to everyday life helps achieve this healing. The shiva was the worst period; the shloshim was very difficult, and the third stage is still bad. In time, it will get better.

STAGE THREE: THE ONE-YEAR PERIOD

UNVEILING

The erecting of a tombstone gives honor to the body that housed the soul. No tombstone is placed at the time of burial.[11] Rather, the Jewish custom is to erect the stone at a later date. Some people do it as early as right after the shiva, while others wait to do it sometime within the year.[12]

Recently the ceremony called *hakamat matzeivah* (the raising up of a stone) has been referred to as an "unveiling." Those close to the family are invited to the grave site where the mourners unveil the stone covered by a cloth.

The ceremony is usually short; psalms are recited, and people often share thoughts about the deceased. The following ideas will contribute to an understanding of this important custom. They could be shared at an unveiling ceremony.

The Hebrew word for stone is *tzur*. This word is also used to refer to God. At this time of remembrance, we remind ourselves that God is our rock, our strength, and support. He is our one constant, always there to comfort us at our darkest times.

A stone is also symbolic of eternity, like the cornerstone of a building, placed to last for all time. And what is eternal about our loved ones? It is their lasting qualities that we can still rely on. Our loved ones live on because they affected us on the deepest of levels. We erect stones and remember what they erected in their lifetimes—their deeds, their character. They will never be forgotten.

A person is created *tzelem Elokim* (in the image of God). This is not a physical image but an image that is internal and ultimately eternal: a person's soul.[13]

VISITING THE CEMETERY

Although a person can visit the cemetery any time after the stone is erected, special days are assigned for visiting the grave:[14]
- On the seventh day after ending the restrictions of shiva
- On the conclusion of the shloshim, the thirtieth day of mourning
- On the completion of the first twelve months of mourning
- On the yahrtzeit, the anniversary of the death, every year

Many people also visit graves the day before Rosh Hashanah and the day before Yom Kippur. Why these days? These are all naturally reflective times, when a person is focused on what is really important in life. Visiting the grave of a loved one opens our minds and hearts and makes us realize that we need help in many aspects of our lives. We pray to God at these times and ask our loved one to be an advocate to Him on our behalf.[15]

You may have noticed that the Jewish custom is not to bring flowers to the grave but instead to place a simple stone on the gravestone itself. Rabbi Abner Weiss, in his book *Death and Bereavement*, states that flowers have no place in a contemporary Jewish funeral and are considered an unconscionable waste of money. Instead, money should be given in the deceased person's memory to tzedakah (charity). Flowers do nothing for a departed loved one, while acts of merit, such as giving tzedakah, help elevate the person's soul.

We give honor to the body with a proper funeral only as recognition that the body had sanctity because it housed and served the *neshama* (the soul). In the same way, the casket should be plain and simple and the money allocated instead to spiritual matters that will affect the person's soul.

We place a small stone on the gravestone as a sign that we were there—not so the person who passed away will know, for the *neshama* already has awareness, but so that we will know. We who are physical need physical acts to express the reality that we were indeed there. The stone is the calling card of the visitor. Flowers die, but the small, simple stone, a symbol of eternity, represents our eternal devotion to upholding the memory of our beloved. Our connection lives on and will never die.

During the twelve-month period from the day of death (which includes the shiva and shloshim), only one who has lost a parent is still considered a mourner after the first thirty days, with the restrictions discussed below. Why this extra stage of mourning only for a parent?

Psychologically and spiritually, our connection to our parents is the essential relationship that defines who we are as people. Therefore, the loss of a parent requires a longer period of adjustment.

This period of time guides us into a deep state of gratitude to our parents for all that they gave and all that they did. As children, we spend most of our lives in a "taking mode," and our parents, being parents, are almost constantly in a "giving mode." It is hard to say thank you from a taking perspective (that is why it's hard for our children to say thank you). In the relationship in which it is the most difficult to show gratitude, this mourning period helps us to focus on recognizing the good that they desperately tried to give in the best way that they could.

Parents also represent values and ideals. They are God's representatives to us in this world. They try to impart in their own way essential tools for living. This extended period of mourning recognizes that the loss of such a relationship has deep spiritual ramifications.

After the shloshim period, life slowly begins to return to normal. Social engagements are allowed, but the pursuit of entertainment and amusement, especially where music is involved, is curtailed. One is allowed to actively engage in business activities. After the year is complete, one is not considered a mourner.

YAHRTZEIT

Each year on the yahrtzeit, the Jewish anniversary of the death of a loved one, a proper commemoration should take place. If you are not sure of the Jewish date, contact a synagogue, *yeshiva,* or the funeral home you used when your loved one died and somebody will surely help you. Some people are careful to perform the following observances:

- Light a yahrtzeit candle at home the night before because the Jewish day begins in the evening.
- Give tzedakah in memory of the loved one.
- Learn Torah that day—read from a book about Judaism or Torah ideas or arrange to learn with someone from the community.
- Recite Kaddish or, if you cannot, arrange for someone to recite it on your behalf. Call a local synagogue or *yeshiva* for help.
- Sponsor a kiddish in synagogue on that day or on the Shabbat that falls at the end of that week.
- Fast from sunrise to sunset.

It's significant to note that in Judaism we downplay birthdays, never commemorating the date of birth of one who has passed away, yet we are careful to mark the anniversary of someone's death.

The Talmud describes the custom of celebrating birth using the image of a ship. How odd, it relates, that people hold a big party when the ship is about to sail, yet when it arrives at its destination, nothing is done. It really should be the other way around. Although the day of our birth holds all the potential for the life that will be, the day we die is the marker of who we actually became. Our worth is measured according to how much of our potential was realized. Did we live up to who we were to the best of our ability in the time that we had?

When our loved ones die and go back to God, to their "home port," we mourn not having them here with us, yet we remember what they were able to accomplish in this life. The yahrtzeit's annual commemoration is a time to feel sadness but also to celebrate who a loved one was and the life that he or she lived.

YIZKOR

Yizkor means "remembrance" and is marked with ceremony at the services held in synagogues on significant holidays:[16]

- Yom Kippur
- The last day of Passover
- The last day of Shavuot
- The eighth day of Sukkot (Shemini Atzeret)

We stop to remember on these major holidays because the holidays are expressions of Am Yisrael (the Jewish nation) celebrating together. As a part of the Jewish people, each of us realizes that we are only here as Jews because of those who came before us, who made the decision to be Jews even in the face of great personal risk. The connection to generations past and loved ones gone is made at Yizkor.

In some synagogues, before the private Yizkor prayers, the congregation as a whole recites Yizkor for those who perished in the Holocaust and for the soldiers who gave their lives for the State of Israel.

On the night before these days, when ushering in the holiday, one should light a yahrtzeit candle at home in memory of the loved one (a small candle that burns continuously for approximately 26 hours—available at any Jewish bookstore or grocery).[17]

On the day of Yizkor, one should attend services in the morning. Part way through the service, those who have never been mourners will be asked to leave the sanctuary, while those who have sat shiva in the past will remain.[18] Often someone will speak briefly about remembering, and then all recite prayers in personal tribute to their loved ones.

We ask God to remember them (not that He would forget), and we ask that in return for our devotion and generosity, God would recognize the new source of merit for the soul whose memory is now influencing our conduct.

After the holiday is complete, be sure to give tzedakah, a charitable donation, in your loved one's memory.

GRIEF AND BEREAVEMENT

The process of mourning is not easy, and the Jewish way provides a structure to let mourners feel their aloneness, separating them from the outside world and then gradually reinstating them with people and society. People left on their own after experiencing a tremendous loss come face to face with their own mortality. They realize that life is transient. The heaviness of this reality could cause a person to retreat from people and life.

The laws and customs surrounding the mourning process at first force mourners to separate and feel the pain, but then the traditions take them by the hand and slowly, with meaning, lead them back into life.

When interviewing people who shared their grieving experiences with me, the feeling that I heard expressed time and time again was an overwhelming sense of emptiness. The pain of that emptiness was almost too much to bear.

Rabbi Samson Raphael Hirsch, in his timeless work *Horeb*, speaks about this. He says that when people are in a state of grief, they physically feel a vacuum within them. This is the most painful state a human being can be in because the essential drive of every person is the drive for fullness and completion.

The different stages of mourning allow us to come to grips with the loss. Eventually we realize that the empty hole is not nearly as deep or as vast as we initially felt.

Time does heal. But not because we are busy and the memories fade. With time comes objectivity. We realize that the person we are now is the product of the loved one that we lost. Elements of our character, our actions, and our values all result from this special soul and the experience of loss.

The body, being finite, does die. Yet the soul, the essence of our loved one, is eternal. The connection between us lives on. This reality begins to slowly fill the vacuum, but not completely. We can never fully grasp the eternity of the soul. We will always have that space inside. We are human beings, who are limited in our capacity to truly understand the ways of God and the hereafter.

Not until we ourselves enter that world beyond and are reunited with our loved ones will we truly understand.

Section Four:

Questions People Ask

*I*n this section you'll find quick answers to the many questions you may have about death, burial, shiva, mourning, and the afterlife. These are questions we often hear from people who are grieving or simply curious about what Judaism has to say about these important ideas. The answers are grouped into three sections: "The Ten Most Commonly Asked Questions about Burial, Shiva, and Mourning"; "The Ten Most Commonly asked Questions about Death"; and "The Ten Most Commonly Asked Questions about the Afterlife." You'll find more information about these subjects throughout the book.

THE TEN MOST COMMONLY ASKED QUESTIONS ABOUT BURIAL, SHIVA, AND MOURNING

1. What does the Chevra Kadisha do?

The Jewish burial society (the Chevra Kadisha) provides a valuable and critical service to the Jewish community. Those who serve on the Chevra Kadisha do not do it for fame and fortune. They are special volunteers who have a certain calling to this mitzvah of preparing the dead for burial.

The laws of preparation are very detailed and specific. Please take comfort in knowing that those who are preparing your loved one for burial are doing it with sensitivity and are taking the greatest care to respect the dignity of the departed. They are also acting with a deep sense of spiritual commitment to the entire process. They carefully and respectfully cleanse the body and then cover it in a special burial shroud. They are called day and night to perform this act and rarely receive any recognition for it.

2. What are the most important things to know about burial?

- Cremation is forbidden in Jewish law. The body, intact, must go back to the earth.

- A casket should be as simple as possible—ideally a plain, unvarnished pine box. This symbolizes the fact that we leave this world and all its materialism behind. All we take with us is our deeds. Don't let any funeral director try to convince you that the more you loved the person, the more you should spend on a casket. If you want to do something of value for your loved one, give the money you save on a casket to tzedakah (a Jewish charity) in his or her memory.

- We do not have "open casket" ceremonies. We do not put makeup on the bodies, embalm them, or dress them in the clothing of this world. When people have died, we need to let them go. Putting makeup on them, viewing them as if they were alive, or embalming to preserve them are ideas antithetical to Judaism. Your loved one is not a body but a soul. Trying to hold on to the body misdirects everyone's focus to what is physical instead of what is spiritual. In Israel, caskets are not used. The person is wrapped in the burial shroud and placed directly into the ground.

- Those who come to the funeral to comfort the mourners should actively participate in the burial itself. We are supposed to bury our own. Participation is called a *chessed shel emet*, a "kindness of truth". It is an act of giving on the purest level, for the one you are burying can never do anything for you. This task is painful and it takes time, but it is very important. The casket should be completely covered with earth. This is done by the friends and family of the direct mourners, not the mourners themselves. And then Kaddish is said by the mourners.

  The first shovelful (usually placed by the rabbi or the one conducting the service at the graveside), is made with the back of the shovel, to symbolize that we are not trying to do this in the most efficient physical way. We are here to do the mitzvah of burial, not to fill a hole in the ground.

Following Kaddish the direct mourners leave, and those who have come to the burial stay behind to finish the burial. The earth should now completely fill the grave, to the point where a small mound is seen at the top, differentiating it from the flat ground around it.

3. Must I sit shiva for the full seven days?

The word *shiva* comes from the word *sheva*, which means seven. Seven is a very significant number in Judaism. God created the world in seven days. The seventh day is Shabbat, the holy Sabbath. Seven signifies completion in this world. Observing the shiva for the proper seven days signifies that your loved one completed his or her lifetime in this world. As mourners, we sit and mourn for the full seven days in order to begin the completion of the initial stages of grief and healing. A complete seven-day shiva brings the most difficult period to an end and also builds a bridge to slowly return to our daily lives.

4. Where is the best place to hold the shiva?

If possible, the optimum place to have the shiva is at the home of the departed. If necessary, those who are required to sit shiva can do so in more than one place. Often a sibling must return home to another city following the burial and can sit shiva away from the rest of the family. The ideal is to be together, but that is not always possible.

5. Must I provide food and beverages for those coming to pay a shiva call?

No. Do not turn the shiva into a party. Food and drinks create a festive atmosphere that you want to avoid. Friends and loved ones who want to send food should do so for the direct mourners, not for those coming to comfort the mourners.

6. Are people supposed to come to the shiva at any time, day or night?

It is permissible to have specific hours for the shiva that can be announced at the funeral and posted on the door of the shiva house.

7. Must we have services at the shiva house?

The best practice is to have prayer services so that the direct mourners can say Kaddish with a *minyan* (prayer quorum). Three services are held each day: Shacharit (morning), Mincha (afternoon), and Maariv (evening). The latter two are usually held together, with Mincha just before sundown, followed by a short break during which someone can speak about the departed. Then Maariv immediately follows. If it is not possible to have all the services, try to hold at least one of them so that Kaddish is said daily.

8. What if I can't say Kaddish every day for the eleven months required of me?

Kaddish must be said for the departed. It is required for thirty days following the burial for everyone except a parent. If a parent passes away, his or her children must say Kaddish daily for eleven months. If it is not possible to do this, or if you know that it will not be done on certain days, you can give tzedakah to someone to say it on your behalf.

We recommend that people contact Aish HaTorah in Jerusalem to arrange for a rabbinical student to say Kaddish at the Western Wall. This sponsors him in his studies and is a special way for you to remember your loved one and ensure that a proper Kaddish is always said. You can go to www.aish.com and click on "Kaddish" on the left-hand side of the page. Aish HaTorah will also make sure that Kaddish is said on every yahrtzeit (the annual anniversary of the death) of the departed.

9. I know I should avoid musical and festive events during the year of mourning. But what if I am invited to a wedding?

You can attend the wedding ceremony but not the reception. If it is very, very important for you to attend the reception because of the nature of your relationship with the family of the bride and groom, then you must be part of the staff, so to speak, in order to attend. That means you must be a temporary waiter or waitress so that you are working and not just attending.

10. If I am married to one who is a direct mourner, what is my role in the process?

You do not sit shiva, and you are not restricted by the laws of the stages of mourning. You simply need to be respectful and behave in a manner that is appropriate for the situation involving a loss and for the overall feeling in the house of mourning.

THE TEN MOST COMMONLY ASKED
QUESTIONS ABOUT DEATH

1. I understand you are supposed to be with people when they die and not leave them alone until the burial. Why is that?

A person has a body and a soul. The body is temporary while the soul is eternal. At the moment of death, though the soul leaves the body, it remains close to the body and does not completely leave this world until after the burial itself. You stay with the person in order to comfort the soul.

2. Why is the soul still here?

Judaism doesn't teach that the body is bad, the soul is good, and the two do battle with one another throughout life. The body and soul are supposed to be a team, led by the soul. Together they make the best decisions so the individual can realize his or her potential. This partnership causes the soul to become attached to the body, and only when the earth covers the coffin does the soul depart this world.

3. What if no one is present when somebody dies?

God, in His infinite wisdom, decides how and when a person should die. Many people have shared stories with me of how they and their siblings were with a dying parent around the clock and yet the parent passed away in a brief moment when no one was there.

The will to live is incredibly strong. And sometimes when a life is really at its end, we have to give our loved ones permission to let go and to leave this world. Often people who are dying know, on a deep level, how painful it will be for those left behind, and they can only let go when they are alone, sparing those they love the pain of witnessing their last breath.

Do not feel bad about not being there. Somehow, it was meant to be.

4. How can someone possibly be with a person around the clock until the burial?

The Chevra Kadisha (burial society) of a community can arrange for a series of shomrim (literally, "guards") to be with your loved one around the clock. Each shomer should be Jewish.

5. Does a person who is in a coma have awareness of what is happening around him or her?

Take comfort in knowing that although the body may be suffering, the person's soul is not. And that soul has complete awareness of what is happening. Anyone who works in hospice care will tell you that you should always speak and conduct yourself around a person who is dying with the knowledge that he or she has awareness. The soul is trapped inside this body that is breaking down, preparing for the end. Thus you can ask the person's forgiveness, speak loving words, and even give the person permission to depart.

6. What else should I do if I am with a person who is at the end?

The last thing on our lips before we depart this world should be the definitive Jewish statement that captures the core meaning of our very existence. The statement is known as the Shema:

Shema Yisrael, Adonai Eloheinu, Adonai Echad.

Hear O Israel, the Lord is God, God, the One and Only.

Ideally, people who are dying should say the Shema themselves. If they are unable, you can say it for them.

7. Is it true that one should make a "deathbed" confession?

A person wants to leave this world with a clean slate. That means making peace with those the person may have had conflict with and also making peace with God. This process is called teshuvah, which means "return." (See Day Twenty in section 2 for the steps of teshuvah.) Ideally, a person should say the *viduy*, the confessional prayers that are said on Yom Kippur. If the person who is at the end of life is in a weakened state or is not accustomed expressing spiritual ideas and feelings, encourage him or her to say the following prayer:

I acknowledge before You, Hashem, my God and God of my fathers, that my recovery or death is in Your hands. May it be Your will that You heal me completely; but if I die, may my death be an atonement for all the mistakes, sins, and rebellions I have erred, sinned, and rebelled before You. May my portion be in Gan Eden, and may You allow me to be in the World to Come, which lies in store for the righteous.

8. If my loved one's soul is going on to a better place, then is it wrong to be sad?

Our sadness and despair have to do with our loss, not the journey of the person departing. The sadness you feel is normal and part of the healthy mourning process that one needs to go through. The fact that your loved one is going on to a place of clarity and harmony, where ultimately no pain or struggle exists, should bring you comfort. This does not remove the pain and sadness, but it should lessen it and help carry you through the critical stages of mourning.

9. Can I communicate with my loved one after death?

It seems that communicating with the dead is possible but, in Jewish law, forbidden. Several commandments address the idea of communing with the dead, but all strictly forbid a Jew from doing so.[1] You want your loved ones to be free to go on to the next world and bask in all the soul-filled pleasures offered there. Contact draws them back to this world and detains them from the pleasure in heaven. Let them go, for their sake and for yours. Give the mourning process more time; you will heal.

10. Is death a punishment?

Basically, no reward and punishment is in place in this world. Only in the World to Come does that reward and punishment set in. Death is not a punishment; it is a guarantee. We are dying from the moment we are born. But often we mistakenly interpret an early death as a punishment and a long life as a reward.

"Everyone knows they are going to die, but no one believes it," says Morrie in *Tuesdays with Morrie*.[2]

We come into this world as if we had little backpacks on our backs. Each has a number signifying how many years we are destined to live. Some say 7, some say 37, and some say 107. But only God can see the number.

Clearly in the Torah, our forefathers and foremothers had years added and years taken away based on the choices that they made, but because they had spiritual clarity back then, people knew when time was added or subtracted and why.[3] Today we do not know the original number we were given, and thus we cannot have the clarity to know if we were given more years or if years were taken away.

Imagine you go to the shiva of someone who died very young, perhaps at twenty-seven. Everyone is devastated. But it may be that her backpack had originally said 7, and for some reason she was granted twenty more years. And if you go to the shiva of someone who was eighty-seven, you are likely to say, "At least he lived a long life." But what if his backpack originally said 107 and for some reason twenty years were taken away?

We simply can't know all of the considerations that determine when a person's life will or will not end: reward, punishment, our personal mission in life; the impact we may be having on others, the impact others have on us. This is where trusting in God comes in. He knows the number, He knows the plan, and He sees a picture that is far bigger than any we can imagine. We are always in His hands.

THE TEN MOST COMMONLY ASKED QUESTIONS ABOUT THE AFTERLIFE

1. Does Judaism believe in the existence of heaven and hell?

Yes, but the afterlife is not full of angels with wings and devils with pitchforks. While alive we live in a state of conflict—a conflict between body and soul. When we live a soul-driven life, the soul is strengthened and elevated. When we live a physically centered, body-driven life, the soul is weakened, tarnished, and even wounded. Hell (in Hebrew, Gehenom), is a "hospital for the soul." We are thankful we have hospitals in this world, but we never want to need one. We know that hospital stays are difficult and very painful. Nonetheless, if we do need surgery, we are grateful that hospitals and their medical teams are available. This is how it is with Hell. That He created a place where spiritual wounds can be healed is an expression of God's kindness and love. If we didn't correct our mistakes and properly care for our souls while alive, we can take care of them there.

The maximum time you can be in Hell is for the 12 months of a Jewish year. (We say Kaddish for eleven months because we would never assume the departed person needs the elevation and healing for an entire year.)

Heaven is a world of incredible spiritual pleasure for healthy souls. It is often compared to a theater. Imagine God is center stage. Being close to him is the ultimate pleasure. Everyone has a seat in the theater, but some sit in the front row center, some sit in the balcony, and others have an obstructed view. Your seat and pleasure in heaven is based on the choices you made in this world.

For more about Heaven and Hell, see section 1.

2. Does Judaism believe in reincarnation?

Yes, but coming back again isn't the ideal. It means you didn't get life right the first time around and you still have important work to do. Reincarnation is for rectification. You can come back with a different gender, with a different religion, or even belonging to a different species. It's even possible to return as an inanimate object.

When a soul does come back, it's not exactly the same soul. A soul that returns with another body is like a candle lit from another candle. The second flame is an extension of the first, and it only exists because of the first, yet it has its own separate identity and it in no way diminishes the first flame.

3. I heard that Judaism believes in the resurrection of the dead. What's that all about?

Resurrection is one of the cornerstones of Jewish belief. Judaism believes that one day the Messiah will come and usher in a new, more spiritually refined and morally attuned era. Then, about a thousand years after the Messiah comes, the world will be transformed into a qualitatively different place. All souls will be judged for a final time, and God will decide who merits eternity and who does not. If you merit eternity, your body and soul will be reunited and live once again. Resurrection of the dead is that reunification of the body and soul. Is this a wild idea? You bet. But God can do anything.

What will someone look like at the time of resurrection—if she was old when she died, will she start out again as an old woman? If you had one leg, would you still have one leg?

Your body will be a reflection of your soul's accomplishments in this world. If your soul achieved great things, then your body will reflect that for eternity—you will look just great! On the other hand, if you devoted most of your time, money, and effort to your body and not a lot to your soul, then your body will reflect that too—forever.

4. Where does the Messiah fit in to all of this?

The Messiah is a uniquely great leader and a mortal human being. The Messiah can come because the world is so spiritually refined and morally elevated that it deserves such leadership or because the world is so debased that only such a leader could save it. If he comes because of the latter condition, it will mean a war of all wars, but this will ultimately end and the world will be permeated with the awareness of God.

5. What does Judaism say about near-death experiences?

The Talmud mentions the phenomenon of near-death experiences.[4]

There is nothing like a near-death experience to wake you up to life. Countless people have told me amazing stories of their near-death experiences, and a pattern can be seen in all of them. People feel a sense of calm, and then they have an out-of-body experience. They watch themselves going through the trauma and everyone around trying to help. They usually feel drawn to a white light in a calm and peaceful way. Yet, for some reason, they do not fully proceed into the light. Abruptly, they return.

The experience is profoundly life changing. People who have gone through it are refocused on their life here, realizing they have been given a second chance. They also do not have a fear of death as they know it is beautiful, natural, and truly "life after life."

6. Are deceased relatives aware of what I am doing here?

Our departed loved ones do have awareness of the spiritual dimension of the world they left behind. They know when *mitzvot* (commandments) are obeyed in this world; they know when we live our lives differently because of how they lived and because they died.

Our loved ones have this awareness because those events change their place in the World to Come. They "move up rows," so to speak, in the theater of heaven. What we do in this world counts, not only for ourselves but for our loved ones who have passed. We only exist because they existed. We are here because of the choices they made. Likewise, our choices have an impact on them.

7. Is it possible to contact the dead?

Yes, but it is completely forbidden in Judaism.[5] We want the deceased to separate from this world and travel to the highest part of heaven. By communicating with them, we draw them back to this world and interfere with their journey. Although wanting to contact them is selfish on our part, it is understandable. We so desperately miss them. Please know that if you truly love them, you will let them go. Cherish their memory and elevate their souls by doing what is right in this world. That is what they want you to do. That is what is right to do.

8. When people die, are they reunited with family and friends?

In the next world, you have awareness of and a connection to your loved ones. For couples, the way they relate to one another—care for and love one another—has a particularly profound impact on how they will spend eternity. This is because when two people marry they become one soul, and in the next world you exist as a soul. Apparently the quality of your eternity is largely based on how you treat your spouse in this world. So choose your spouse wisely, and work very hard at your marriage. Marriage is not just for now; it's for eternity.

9. If I see a departed relative in a dream, does that mean anything?

Dreams are significant but not easy to understand. The Talmud says that a portion of dreams is prophecy and a portion is nonsense.[6] The problem is that it's hard to know which is which. We are supposed to always interpret dreams in a positive manner, for if it is a prophetic dream, it will be fulfilled according to the interpretation. If you have a recurring dream, you should take it seriously and perhaps discuss it with a rabbi who can help you understand its meaning. A recurring nightmare may be a message to change your ways and do teshuva (see Day Twenty in section 2). In this case, you are advised to seek the guidance of a rabbi.

10. Does Judaism allow for cremation?

No, cremation is strictly forbidden. The body has sanctity because it housed the soul. We treat the body with great respect. We are commanded to return our bodies to the earth, for that is where, in the beginning, they came from (Adam was formed from the earth). And, as we have discussed in question 3 above, one day you are going to need your body again.

Section Five:

Reflections:
Looking Back on the Loss of a Loved One

Most of the people who agreed to be interviewed for this book were not religiously observant at the time of their losses. Some, since that time, have become more observant, and some have not. The feelings they shared with me were heartfelt and real. It was not easy for them to relive one of the most painful periods in their lives, but they did. I will be forever grateful to them.

(Note: The following reflections are personal memories of those who have lost a loved one and are not intended as a halachic guide to the laws of mourning. To ensure privacy, all names have been changed.)

Steve, forty-three, lawyer
Lost his father to leukemia nine years ago

When I knew my father's life was nearing the end, I tried to find a rabbi to come to the hospital. I don't know why I felt it was important. He didn't make it in time, so it was all up to me.

The nurse said I should go in and say good-bye to him and that even though his body was letting go, listening becomes very acute at the end and he would hear me. So I did just that. I went in and said good-bye to my father for the last time.

Everything became very surreal from that point on. His breathing became very labored. I was holding his hands. And then the long breath came, and he died.

This may sound strange, but at the time I felt as if a presence had left his body and shifted to another place. I knew his spirit or soul was outside of him looking down at me. (This was before I had ever learned that in Judaism that is exactly what takes place.) I felt he was part of the room, his presence was so "there." I didn't know what to do, so I said the Shema, said good-bye, told him he was a good father, and cried.

Going to the funeral home was strange. They lead you into a room and you go shopping for a coffin. I remember they got the contact person at the cemetery on the speakerphone and he said, "Have I got a spot for you!"

The funeral was surreal, that is the only way to describe it. Time wasn't normal time anymore. Everything happened in slow motion. You're there in your body, but your consciousness is moving at a different speed. I remember feeling as if I was the luckiest guy in the world because my wife worked at a center for Jewish learning and all the rabbis came. They made sure everything was done properly, and long after we had left the grave site, they were still there shoveling and completing the burial. Without their support, I never would have been able to conduct a proper shiva. I didn't feel lost in space. I felt comforted and part of a family. I kept thinking how lucky I was not to be left alone with just an obligatory visit from a representative from a synagogue. I was fortunate in an unfortunate situation.

My father was the first one of his generation in the family to die, and it seemed strange that this whole event fell upon me. I remember my cousins commenting how well I was handling it, that I was doing things right. That made me feel good.

During the shiva I kept thinking how much it all made sense—that this age-old ritual jibes so well with a modern healing process. When you get up at the end and walk around the block for the first time in a week—that's right out of EST or something. It felt so good.

Saying Kaddish every day was incredible. I hadn't used my Hebrew since my *bar mitzvah*, and it came back to me and really improved. What's more amazing is that years later I found myself able to sit down with my son and help him with his Hebrew studies because of it—and that's the son who's named after my father.

Kaddish made me feel spiritual. I realize that the experience isn't over just because I may not have the outer signs of observance. I carry my father's death with me every day of my life.

My attitude toward everything has changed—children, life, death. At least once a day I think about, God forbid, what if I weren't here? This fear of death is a recurring nightmare.

I believe there is another realm, but I don't know. It's not comforting when I think about what's going to go on up there. I think about it all the time, whether my father is watching me. Sometimes I wish it weren't true, because there are things I'd be more embarrassed to do in front of my father than in front of God. You'd like to think you can fool your father when you're growing up, but you can't fool God. Now my father is up there seeing it all too.

My own fear of death is not for myself so much, but for my kids. I don't want them to have to go through life without us. I hear about people dying in a bus accident, leaving children behind, and I ask, "Why God, why?"

I bought this great book, *The Jewish Way in Death and Mourning* by Maurice Lamm, and on the first day of the shiva I read the rules to my family. They appreciated it. The shiva was happening in my house, and everyone knew how it was going to be conducted. Knowledge is soothing.

We had the classic family shiva experiences—people who had been fighting for twenty-five years still fighting. At one point I had to leave the house to convince my aunt to come back in.

Some stupid and annoying things happened during the shiva. One day a bunch of women who were interior decorators came in, friends of my wife's mother. They sat down and started talking about carpeting and draperies. I couldn't take it and said something like, "Not now!" and got up and walked out. I really wanted to say, "Shut up! My father died. I don't want to hear this."

One funny thing happened. Two sisters about seventy-five years old came every night during the week of shiva. No one knew who they were. They came, they ate, and they left, every night. We used to say to each other, "Oh, the girls are here."

The people I thought I was close to often were the ones who didn't know how to comfort me properly. I was disappointed. But one old friend, who had always come across as kind of distant, came and immediately put his arms around me and said, "You don't have to say anything." It was a moment that deeply comforted me. Maybe it was because I hadn't expected that of him, but even years later I feel very moved when I think about it.

I committed to saying Kaddish for the eleven months for my father. It was a sacrifice for me because I'm not a *shul* (synagogue) person. Because of that I knew that making the effort and doing it in his memory would make him proud.

I liked going to different synagogues and seeing the people come and go. It was like a club and it was comforting—not "misery likes company." It was a support group. I had no clue how to put on *tefillin* or say Kaddish, and I met a guy who had lost his wife and he taught me how to do it all. You would go in, see friendly faces, say Kaddish, have some breakfast, you knew you were part of a community. I said it on trips, at the cottage, everywhere.

I knew I would say Kaddish for my father when he died long before he was even sick. Before I was married, I remember getting dressed to go out and the television was on. It was a movie about the war. In the scene were two men in a concentration camp. One was a Jew, and one was not. The Jew was an older man, and he told the younger one that what bothered him the most was that because the Nazis had killed his whole family, when it was his time there would be no one to say Kaddish for him.

The non-Jew said, "Teach it to me and I will say it for you." And he did.

I sat down on my bed and cried. The scene was so moving. It always stayed with me.

At the end of the eleven months I felt that this religion was brilliant. It fits into modern psychology, and it eased me through this horrible period of my life.

I don't go to the cemetery as much as I used to. I don't know what I'm supposed to do there. I feel awkward and I don't know how to make my visit meaningful. It feels artificial, imposing. The time there is too short, too brief. To feel close to my father, all I have to do is sit and think or hold my kids. I have his arms; they're hairy, just like his. So when I throw my kids in the air in the pool, just as he did with me when I was little, I see them laughing, I see my arms, and I am filled with my father.

When I am in a synagogue where I said Kaddish for my father, I feel close to him. That's my connection to Judaism—past generations, who we are.

The saddest thing is that my kids don't know him. Worse is that he didn't know them. They were born after he passed away.

I don't fault God for taking my father. I believe in God, but it's a tricky concept. I know the soul lives on.

I gave tzedakah to the Jewish learning center for a tape library in my father's honor. I suppose I should get a yahrtzeit plaque for the new *shul* that I belong to. And I think I should tell my friend who hugged me at the shiva how much it meant to me then and still does.

Stacey, thirty-three, homemaker
Lost her grandfather twelve years ago

I lost my grandfather when I was in my twenties. He was in his seventies, and I was very close to him. He had just recovered from a broken hip after a fall on the ice and then suddenly had a heart attack and died.

My first thoughts were shock—why such a good man, and why so soon? Then it was just grief. He was the favorite of all of my grandparents, and I felt very alone when he left. I kept asking myself, did he know that I loved him? Did I tell him enough? When was the last time I told him?

I don't even remember those first hours. I must have been in shock.

The funeral was awful for my mom. She turned to me and said, "I'm an orphan now." I just remember a lot of gut-wrenching tears. Even though it was hard, it felt good being surrounded by all the aunts, uncles, and family.

The actual burial was bad. The sound of the first earth hitting the coffin is the hardest sound—it cracks right through you. I regret that we didn't stay to completely fill the grave ourselves.

I remember thinking that it was a very pretty cemetery. I thought he'd be happy here next to his wife.

My mother and I grieved together—he was her father. Throughout the shiva, we just shadowed each other, as if we couldn't stay alone. We needed that closeness. A lot of people came, a lot of friends. Throughout the week I found myself talking to him, telling him, "Look who showed up. Look at all that food." My grandfather was always an "up" guy, always looking at the bright side of life. After a family meal he would say, "That was the best meal ever!" I knew he was looking down that week and saying, "That's the best buffet I've ever seen at a shiva!"

My mother has a hard time with death, so she didn't sit a full week.

The stupidest thing someone said to me at the shiva was, "Was it expected?" His death was sudden, but even if someone is hooked up to life support for six months, death is never expected.

The most comforting thing that week was a visit from a man up the street who had just lost his three-year-old daughter. He spoke about her being in Heaven. He was also listening to my mom. The thought of him giving to us while going through his own grief was so touching.

My mom also had a friend who came every day at three. You don't realize how you need people when you are going through grief. Your first instinct is to withdraw.

The funniest thing happened when we went together to clean out his apartment. My grandfather always traveled with his stuff in boxes with everything bundled and tied with rubber bands. I joked to my Mom that that's exactly what we'd probably find, and sure enough, we found a box— filled with rubber bands! We couldn't stop giggling.

The saddest thing for me was that my husband never got to meet him. My wedding was bittersweet because he wasn't there.

I feel closest to my grandfather around his birthday. It's been twelve years, but I still have some of his sweaters, and one of them I still wear. I wore it the other day, and I told Mom it was Grandpa's. She said, "Let me smell it." I told her his smell wouldn't be there. So she gave it a kiss.

I also think of him whenever anyone takes a picture. He used to take a half-hour to focus his camera, and it would make everyone crazy.

I tell my son that he is named after his great-grandfather, but it's so sad that he'll never get to know him. You know, I never feel very far away from him. He's not here physically, but he's here. A light went out when he died, but I know he's in another place. I feel connected to him and very much felt his presence at my wedding and at the *brit* of our first son, who was named for him. My son is actually very much like him: so sweet, a good listener, and a great talker. At the *brit* I was overwhelmed with feelings. I was honoring my grandfather but wished I didn't have to. I wished that he was standing right beside me. I wished he could hold me instead of the reality—that I was giving someone his name.

If you truly adore someone, you're always connected to that person. I miss him, but still feel a part of him. It's amazing how big a heart can be. Just talking about him now, my heart is swelling.

Sure, I was angry at God when he died, but that's healthy. He's the only One I can yell at. I allow myself to be angry, and then that feeling fades and more of an understanding comes in and an acceptance of the loss.

I see now the purpose of all this. Death wakes you up to life around you. I just wish there were another way.

Stacey, the same woman
Lost a friend at twenty

I had a friend in high school who was a real free spirit. She took off and went to California. She would write to me about what a great time she was having and how she had learned to play the guitar.

One day I was downtown and saw another friend from high school. "How are you doing?" she asked me in a strange way. "Are you going? Didn't you hear?"

My friend's name flashed before me. Even before she told me that she was dead, I knew. Apparently she had been walking along a beach in California and a man attacked and stabbed her and half buried her in the sand.

It was shock, absolute shock.

I got home and told my mom and broke down. At the funeral service, all of us, all her high school friends, were a mess in the back.

On the way to the cemetery, a cop pulled us over for some minor infraction. We explained to him that we were in a funeral procession, but he wouldn't let us go. By the time he wrote out the ticket, all the cars were long gone, and we couldn't find the cemetery. I never got to say good-bye.

The shiva house was unreal. It was such a violent death. I kept thinking, "What were her last thoughts?" The only way to describe it was that she was taken from us.

A letter arrived at my house from her after the funeral. She had obviously written and mailed it just before her death. These were her last words, and she sounded so happy. The letter really freaked me out. It's been almost thirteen years, and I still have that letter today.

I was tormented that I never got to speak to her or say good-bye—and then she came to me in a dream. She looked so pretty. She said, "It's okay. I'm all right. Don't worry." I woke up, and I was at peace.

Donna, thirty-nine, artist
Lost her mother to a heart condition five years ago

My mother was fifty-seven when she died of a heart condition. She was only fifty-seven and looked even younger.

She was lucid until the end, and in the final weeks, it was a miracle that she even hung on. I still remember those calls from the hospital in the middle of the night. We would all rush down, but somehow she made it through.

Before she died, I couldn't even think what life would be like without my parents. I always thought, "How could I survive without my mother and father?" But when it happened, I was surprised that it was so natural. It wasn't the awful nightmare that I had thought it would be. I was grateful that I was able to say good-bye to her.

The immediate hours after her death were so sad, but they flowed. Nothing was hard or unexpected about it. There were practical things to deal with, and we did them. Somehow we got through it. I remember thinking, "I survived." I was still myself. I am still myself. But her death deeply affected me.

The fact that she died young made me question my life. There were things that were not resolved that I finally faced head-on with the motto, "Why wait?" Her death gave me the courage to face a relationship that needed to end, and I was able to move on in my career too. I realized that's all there is in life, so if you don't do something now, you won't do it ever.

In her last days, I wanted to write down every detail—how she looked— everything became so important. I taped her voice in the hospital and was able to record the last few memories.

I hardly remember the funeral. I think I blanked a lot of it out. Afterward I went back to New York and I was in an elevator.

A man came in and said, "You look like you just lost your mother."

"I did," I said. The poor guy. I guess it was all over my face.

I remember that there was a lot of food at the shiva and that my aunt brought some candy. We served it to the people who came, and she got upset that we didn't eat it ourselves. I was so upset—I just lost my mother and all she cares about is the protocol of candy!

I think I was in shock. It took me a long time to cry. I was in a daze and holding myself in. I ask myself now if I really mourned her completely. My father was in total denial. My mother had always been the stronger one. She was the central part of the family, and we fell apart a little after she was gone.

The burial was very hard, watching her being put into the earth. I was imagining how she looked. It was so final.

She died on the second night of Passover, so her yahrtzeit is difficult to focus on. We're all together, which is nice, but we're all so busy.

It's hard for me to connect to Yizkor. I don't usually feel it. Now with the new baby, I usually say it at home. I feel it is very formal, and I'm not emotionally moved by it. In *shul* it is said very fast, and it's hard to get into a state of remembering.

My mother left very few physical things, but I have a tablecloth of hers that I always use, which is almost threadbare. Whenever it is on the table, I feel as if she's touching me and patting me on the back.

And as I get older, I look more and more like her. I'm even getting farsighted like her!

I feel close to her when I see aspects of myself that are like her. We are very different, but the soft part of my personality is from her.

I feel the loss most when something very special happens and she's not there to share it with. I wasn't settled when she died, and I think she would be proud of me now.

I don't feel connected to her in another place, and I don't feel that she sees me. But it's funny: I cut my finger badly the other day. There was a lot of blood, and as I was squeezing it I cried, "Mommy, Mommy, Mommy."

I also inherited her rocking chair, the one she used to rock me in. I have it today and rock my little baby in it. I sing the same song my mother used to sing to me, "Ay la loo baby." Of all the songs that I sing, that's the one my baby loves the most. She asks for "Ay ay, baby."

I felt that God gave me a gift. I was able to spend time with my mother before she died. Her death taught me that life was natural and death was natural. People don't get gobbled up; the body simply shuts down. There is something not jolting about it. Yes, He works the world, and death is part of the way the world works. It made me appreciate that things have a natural flow. Even if someone's death is sudden, God usually makes it seem that somehow it was meant to be that way.

I believe in another world, but I'm not sure. But I think I'll see her again.

I felt that her death gave my life more life. It made me appreciate more what life was about.

The hardest thing is never having that opportunity to see her again. She never met my husband, never saw my daughter who was named for her. She never saw who I became. She never saw me build a Jewish home.

Robert, sixty, accountant
Lost his three-year-old daughter to drowning in 1971

It was her third birthday. She was the youngest of all my children. There was a big family get-together, and somehow everyone thought that someone else was watching her, and she wandered away. I wasn't there. They found her in the pool.

The questions screamed out—Why was she there? She was afraid of water! Other kids were there. Why didn't anyone see her?

But the biggest question was, were was God? Why did He do this to me? It took a long time to get over that one.

It was the Sunday before Labor Day, and being an accountant for my father-in-law's amusement company, I was working. A call came in from my brother-in-law, and my father in-law answered it. He gave it to me. My brother in-law was crying, totally out of control. It happened at his house. My wife was in a state of shock.

I drove the forty-minute drive to their house in twenty minutes. I don't know how I stayed alive. The whole time I was in denial. You hold onto hope. "It must be a mistake. I know she's not dead." By the time I got there, the police had taken her to the morgue and I had to go and identify her and ask them not to do an autopsy.

The next day was the funeral. The Jewish way of structure and immediacy was comforting. There wasn't too much time to think about things. You just do it.

I don't remember the funeral. I was in shock. I just remember crying through the whole thing. I remember the simple casket. I remember people's kindnesses.

The whole Jewish system of mourning brought me through it. My rabbi was a terrific pillar of support. Friends rallied around. Clients sat with us at the shiva, and there was *davening* night and day.

The first two or three nights were nightmares. I don't know how my four other kids dealt with it. I was so immersed in my own suffering. I think they have a better chance to overcome grief than their parents. They went on with their lives. They're not as in touch with their inner thoughts.

Afterward I got my wife a job to get her out of the house, and I buried myself in my work. We didn't pay attention to the family. I couldn't get my wife to grieve openly. She just started working, volunteering. You learn that everyone grieves in his or her own way.

We never talk about it, only on her yahrtzeit and on *yom tov*. When I go to *shul* at those times, I don't feel good. That's why sometimes it's hard to go.

She was beautiful. She would have been the best.

Losing a child is totally different than any other loss. I helped start a group at a children's hospital to help parents and siblings deal with such a loss.

Someone who had lost a daughter to murder sent me a letter and spoke about Heaven. It helped me. I wanted to believe it, but it's hard for me accept. I've had too many traumas in my life. It's hard to see Someone looking down at me, let alone from the Next World. But if you stop to think, there is a God.

But I do feel connected. I feel she's looking out for me. And I'm holding onto that one ray of hope that we will be together one day.

Kaddish helped me. It was a continuation—there was a past, there is a present, and there will be a future. I didn't have to say Kaddish for a year, but I wanted to. Although I wasn't religious, my father was. I think he was proud that I was doing it. Actually, he wouldn't have let me live if I hadn't done it.

On my daughter's yahrtzeit, I go to the cemetery and think. You think of all the plans you had, how everything is down the drain. But you also try to remember the good things from when she was growing up. She was at her brother's *bar mitzvah* when she was two. She was so cute. It got late, and the caterer's son had to take her back to the house for us.

I light a candle, and I go to *shul* and say Kaddish. My father is gone now, but I still do it.

At Yizkor I have mixed feelings about what she could have become. It bothers me. I feel cheated. She was such a beautiful girl, such a beautiful baby.

It's funny. In the bereavement group we started, the non-Jews say that they wish they had our system of mourning, with the shiva and the different stages. It's clear to them that the process is psychologically good.

The groups helped us. We needed to be with other parents who had experienced the loss of a child. Only someone who has been there understands.

One thing I've learned is that people have to grieve in their own way. It's very personal. It's not easy, and with a child it's hard to accept. I don't think you ever accept it.

I do believe that life is not a destination but a journey, a journey to a better place.

Deborah, twenty-three, physiotherapist
Lost a brother ten years ago in a car accident. Her brother was eleven; she was thirteen

It all happened in South Africa. Halley's comet was in the sky, and our whole family (five of us) plus an aunt and two cousins went camping in a park in the north to get the best view. We were all in a minivan.

The holiday was glorious, and my brother, who was eleven, said to my mom at the end, "I've had such a good time. I've never been so happy."

On the way home, we were traveling across soft sand dunes, singing, having a wonderful time. My mom was driving. Eventually I fell asleep.

Suddenly the van started swerving. A tire blew, and my mom lost control. The van flipped over and rolled. The van had no seat belts, so we all tumbled over one another.

Someone said, "Is everyone okay?" And we began to step out.

I was the first to see my brother. His head had been thrown against the van. He had died immediately. My mother became hysterical.

We didn't know what to do. We were in the middle of nowhere. My dad suggested we try and lift the van, but it was a fruitless suggestion. I was so disturbed. Was he really dead?

From somewhere came another van, and we all got in. Someone stayed behind to stay with my brother. The hardest thing was getting in the van and leaving him. We were silent. I knew he was dead. I felt sick, cold, disbelief. My mom had to be sedated. None of the rest of us were hurt except for my cousin, who broke his collarbone.

I began to have flashbacks and horrible feelings of guilt. I used to hang out with the girl cousins and shut him out. We thought we were so cool. We just tolerated him. Any time I was mean or bossy to him came back to me.

Friends flew us back home in their airplane. There was an icy feeling as we entered the house. Everything felt cold.

The shiva was a blur. I remember covering the mirrors, lots of people, lots of food. I was in a cold daze for a day or so—weird, detached.

After two days friends of my parents took us for two hours to their home to play with their kids. I didn't like their kids, and I didn't want to be there. When I got home, I hid in my mom's room. She found me crying hysterically.

We all slept in the same room for nights. I remember waking up to my mom crying. It was hard seeing my parents completely upset. It was an intangible feeling—my pillars were no longer there. They were suffering, and who could take care of them?

The shiva process is good because it forces you to be personally involved. The family is involved in the reality, and the support is there. It makes you confront it all—you're sitting, not distracted. That's why you're there. I see the value in it now, but at the time it was hard.

I remember someone saying at the shiva, "You must be strong for your mom." Yes, I must be, but I was not feeling strong for myself. I felt sorry for my dad. People kept telling him to be a man and be strong for his wife.

Other stupid things people said: "Check your *mezuzahs*." "At least you have two other kids." People kept telling my mom to eat. Leave her alone! I learned, if you don't know what to say, say nothing. But I can empathize. You would think that I would know better what to say now, but I don't.

I was angry with God. I didn't doubt my belief or question my Jewishness, but I just couldn't understand why something so horrible could happen.

My parents joined a bereavement group, which really helped them. They had groups for siblings, but I said, "No!"

The hardest part was not being able to talk to my parents. There was so much pain in their eyes. If they would bring my brother up, I would cringe because even though I wanted to keep his memory alive, I wanted my connection to be private. As I get older, I can talk about it to my parents more.

Afterward some of my parent's friends pretended he never existed, and that was wrong. The most meaningful thing to my mom was when friends would say, "I miss him too."

He was a bright and wonderful person, intelligent, with special energy—the most like my mom. It is beyond belief what she had to go through. After all, she was driving when it happened. There were times she didn't want to get out of bed, but she had a family who needed her.

At the unveiling I felt very connected to him. Actually I felt that way right after he died. I would talk to him, sense his presence. Many times, later, I have felt that he was watching over me. I feel looked after, protected. Things have fallen into place in my life so smoothly that it's not even logical.

At different times I've had different understandings of what is spiritual. I believe sometimes that souls can connect.

Because he is buried in South Africa, I don't get to visit his grave often. But I remember going there after a few years and thinking of the sense of lost potential. "He'd be twenty now," I thought, even though I knew he wasn't meant to live beyond eleven. But it feels like a loss. Reality is weird. Time and defense mechanisms can blur and protect, but when you're standing at a grave, it's very, very real.

I have a strong sense that there is a greater plan, that my brother's death couldn't have been prevented. But why him? Why someone with such potential for the world and for those around him? It's hard to fathom. You just don't know—can't understand.

The whole experience changed my life. I know I'm a completely different person than I would otherwise have been. I don't focus on trivial things. My teenage years were more serious, and I have chosen to work as an occupational therapist with people who are dying. I think it's because losing my brother made dying less scary. It's hard to explain. I'm also a better sister to my other brother.

I think that because I had to contemplate death so young, I am less scared of dying. People don't face it until they're older. It became so real to me so young that it's part of the cycle. It's normal to die.

I had to attend a funeral of a patient I had gotten close to. It was not a Jewish funeral, so there was an open casket. I looked at her body, and it wasn't her. She looked empty like a vessel. Her spirit was who she was. The separation of body and soul is so strong.

It made me understand why we don't bring flowers to a grave site. We don't try and beautify it because we are not visiting the person. We leave a stone to say we were there. It's a beautiful thing. When I'm actually doing that I feel connected to the soul.

I always believed in life after death and another world. I didn't know what Judaism believed, I knew very little about my own religion. Most Jews seem the same way. We know about every "ism" except Judaism.

When people ask how many siblings I have, I always say, "One." After all, at what point in a relationship or friendship do you bring it up? Anybody who is close to me knows. It's a big part of who I am, and people have been so good about it.

At Yizkor I feel really good. It's a special time. I like taking time to fully concentrate. Even in my youth when I was anti-Judaism, it still felt right to do it.

I feel close to my brother at different times. My other brother looks a lot like him, so I sense that part of the brother I lost lives on in the brother I have. I also feel close when I light a yahrtzeit candle or Yizkor candle. And when things are hard or I'm confused, I feel his presence. I get that "guardian angel" feeling.

I feel farthest away from him when I'm living my life superficially, coasting, getting caught up in things that aren't meaningful.

My brother loved cricket and had memorized statistics and the scores of hundreds of games even though he didn't play himself, so my parents established an award that is given at his school for kids who aren't necessarily athletic but make an effort.

I remember the feeling of terror that my other brother wouldn't reach the age of *bar mitzvah*. He did, but the celebration was bittersweet. It was hard for my mom. But we didn't ignore our loss and spoke about him throughout the day.

John, forty-eight, insurance salesman
Lost his older brother to suicide fifteen years ago

My brother was married with kids, a very social guy, yet fifteen years ago he jumped off a bridge and took his own life.

Apparently his government job was in jeopardy and his marriage wasn't happy. And even though he was social, he never talked about himself or personal subjects. Perhaps he had a lot going on inside that we didn't know.

I got the call at 5:45 a.m. from his wife saying that she had found a suicide note from him. In it he said he was going to throw himself off a local bridge. He had made an early tennis appointment with someone for that day, but he never arrived.

I called the police and gave them what information I knew. I quickly got dressed. Twenty minutes later they found him, and he was dead.

Apparently he had walked in the early morning cold the quarter mile to the bridge and jumped. I identified the body and helped his wife arrange the funeral.

I was totally shaken. How terribly wrong I had been in thinking he had the perfect life. I tried to piece it together. Recently we had become closer, and I knew he was disappointed in where he had gone in life, but this?

The hardest thing I've ever had to do in my life was call my parents in Florida and tell them their son was dead. My father sobbed for half an hour, crying, "No, no, no!" I didn't tell them it was suicide until they came up. It was too much to ask of them to travel with the truth.

Nothing is as you think it is. All foundations of my life were wiped away. It was the beginning of my journey back to Judaism.

The funeral was a sham. The rabbi was a joke. He didn't know us and was recommended by a friend. It was only later that I realized how far from Jewish tradition the service was. I remember my father at the grave site just wanting to leave. He couldn't stand having people look at him with such pity. He said, "For the first time in my life I really feel old." He told me, "Never give up. Never despair. Keep fighting."

My mother just kept repeating, "What a waste, what a waste."

The shiva? The rabbi was there. There was food, family, but very little talk about my brother. It was the first shiva I had ever been at, and it was our own. There was a lot of social talk, and I remember my aunt and uncle saying to my mother that they blamed my father because he wasn't close with my brother. No one was comforting my parents or me. There was a complete sense of unreality.

All my sense of direction in what life was all about, what was meaningful, was devastated. I was so into my career, and this made me refocus my life to something that had real meaning.

I said Kaddish for a few months, but I was numb. I didn't know the words, the meaning of those words. I remember running, saying "Shema" again and again, pleading for answers and help.

I decided to get my own life in order. Playtime was over. I wrote down the qualities that I wanted to find in a Jewish woman.

Today the fear in my heart is that the circumstances that allowed this to happen to my brother would somehow occur in my family or for me. I see emptiness, waste, and loss.

On his yahrtzeit I go to *shul*, lay *tefillin* there, and say Kaddish with a *minyan*. I also light a candle. I always spend time with my mother.

I asked a mystic once if what I'm doing is impacting my brother. He said yes.

I stop by the cemetery and say Kaddish two or three times a year. I feel close to him on Yom Kippur during Yizkor. It's something I can do for him.

I didn't blame myself for his death at first, but later I did. If only I had reconnected with my Judaism earlier, perhaps I could have given him some strength and turned around the family. My parents always blamed themselves.

I had never heard anything about Olam Habah, the next world, back then, but I did have a sense of some spirit.

My relationship with God totally changed. My brother's death made me reach out on my hands and knees.

By all appearances I was fine. But my deepest grief was not for him but for myself. Anything I'd thought had value was now empty. The Judaism I had once turned my back on was now set before me filled with meaning. My journey back was slow, one step at a time, and it was the best thing I had ever done. I just wish it hadn't taken this to make it happen.

It's been years, but I think about him every day, especially when I drive by the bridge. His death is always there.

His physical presence is gone, but there is a lump in my throat when I speak of him, and the weight is heaviest on my heart. I stay busy, trying to fill my life with things that are positive.

My greatest regret is not knowing any way to make up for not saying Kaddish fully for both my brother and later my father. But I didn't know.

Karen, fifty, real estate agent
Lost her father to heart failure two years ago

My mother came home and found my father between the doors. She did CPR, but he remained in a coma for four days, and then he died. Although those days were hard, I will always be grateful for that time that allowed all of us to come to grips with his death and to say good-bye.

We never really knew his age. It was about eighty, but he looked much younger. During those four days in the hospital, we brought pictures of the family and put them at the foot of his bed so that the nurses would know what he looked like, know him as a person, not just as a body.

He used to sing me songs when we were little, old Yiddish songs. So for those four days, I sang to him the songs he sang to me.

We were all with him when he took his last breath. We held his head; it was very loving, very peaceful, his passing away.

All of his grandchildren came in and held his hands until the nurse came and took him off the respirator. My first thoughts were that I didn't want him to die. I wanted him to live.

We came home as a family and were together. It was tough because it was Shabbat and we had to wait to make all the arrangements. What we did then I don't remember.

He was a survivor of the Holocaust, so at the funeral they also paid memory to his first wife and three children, who died during that terrible time. My brother-in-law spoke beautifully and also mentioned the countless cousins that my father lost in the war.

He worked hard, but he didn't care about money. He always said that the only thing that mattered were children and grandchildren.

It rained the day we buried him. It poured all the way to the cemetery, but when we all got there, the rain stopped. It was as if my father didn't want us to get wet. When we got into the car after the burial, it poured again, but as soon as we got to the house, the sun came out.

He used to always say to me "Shluf gezunta heit," (sleep with good health). At the end of the burial, I said those same words to him. "Shluf gezunta heit, Daddy. Shluf gezunta heit."

Hundreds of people came to the shiva, but I didn't want to see anyone; we were all sobbing. I've learned that only those very close should come for the first three days. I understand that now.

At the shiva, Maurice Lamm's book (*The Jewish Way in Death and Mourning*) was like a Bible, guiding us all the way.

My husband led the services at the house, and my son, who had become observant as a kid, spoke words of Torah. I was so proud of all my sons, the way they *davened* in the home.

I remember the meals. There was so much food, but I didn't feel like eating.

I wore the dress that was torn for *kriah* throughout the shiva. People wanted to know why would I allow such a nice dress to be torn? Didn't they know that the dress meant nothing? The tear was like a rip in my heart. When you walk into the shiva, you should know who is hurting.

I hated to hear laughter at the shiva. I thought it was very disrespectful. Until you've lost someone, you don't know. People talked about nonsense; it was very irritating.

It was nice to show people pictures of my father at the shiva.

I felt people were very insensitive. Someone asked me what I was doing in my life in terms of business right now. I also hated it when people stayed on and made the shiva a social event.

The best part was when people shared nice thoughts about my dad, when they shared memories. Everything should be focused on the person who passed away.

I said Kaddish for him for eleven months. At first it made no sense to me. Why was I glorifying God? The Kaddish said nothing about my father. And different Kaddishes were hard to learn. It's hard to praise God for taking him. It's a struggle.

You develop a rapport with others saying Kaddish. When I was away, they would ask where I was—like a Kaddish club. When you are saying it, you realize how precious life is. You are no longer afraid of your own death. It's people around you who matter. It's those you love.

The eleventh month I was in Israel, and my family timed it so that we were all saying the last Kaddish together.

I didn't cut my hair for the shloshim, the first thirty days. I didn't listen to music for a year or go to parties. I didn't watch television or see movies for a year. I felt I needed to do that. I was honoring my father.

I began to learn more about Judaism too, and his death inspired me to be more observant. I made a commitment not to drive on Shabbat in his merit, and even though it was hard, I stuck with it. I gave tzedakah in his name and learned in his memory.

On his yahrtzeit we try and be together as a family and attend services. I learn that day in his memory. I feel sad. I miss him a lot. He always wished everyone the best. He was a real gentleman. A part of me is missing. Whenever I do something positive, I remember it's in his merit.

During Yizkor I miss my dad, and I'm grateful that I am Jewish. And now the Kaddish means more to me. When someone else says it, I answer in response with great respect and support.

I feel closest to him when I'm at a *simcha* that I know he would like. I have his picture framed in my bedroom, and I look at it every day. I feel close to him when I tell my sons to sleep in good health and when I sew my kids' pants (he used to be a tailor) or fix things. When I see the little things he treasured.

I feel far away when a whole day goes by and I haven't thought of him. Sometimes I talk to him.

I visit the cemetery on his yahrtzeit and just before the holidays. Or sometimes I just go. I put a stone on the stone and ask him to intercede with God to give health to the family. I tell him how much I miss him. I know he's in Olam Habah.

I do regret that I didn't spend more time with him, the times that I was too busy and wasn't there for him. But I know he knows how much I love him.

On his stone it says, "If love could save him, he would live forever."

Rebecca, thirty-eight, piano teacher
Lost her father four years ago to a sudden heart attack

My father was a very nonjudgmental person. He never spoke badly about someone; it wasn't in him. He taught me how to enjoy myself and was caring and loving. The childhood memories between a parent and a child stay with you for the rest of your life. The time he took me fishing in the park on Sunday, the museum, swimming. I grew up knowing I was loved.

I got the call that he had had a heart attack and was dead. I rushed right over. I wouldn't let the paramedics take him. I don't know if I knew I had to stay, I just felt I should be with him.

All I could think was, "My father's dead." I was in complete shock. How was I going to cope with this?

The Chevra Kadisha came. It was Shabbat. The funeral homes were closed, so I just sat on the sofa waiting to make the arrangements. My close friends came to see me. The rabbi came and sat and discussed the eulogy. You're not in a normal state of reality. There's a list of things to do, and you don't know what propels you to get through such a crisis. It was very emotional.

At the funeral I saw friends I hadn't seen in years. I was an only child, so I had to go through it alone, but seeing my friends brought my childhood to me.

I don't remember what happened at the cemetery. I've blocked it out.

I said Kaddish for thirty days. It was very healing. I have guilt that I didn't say it for a year. At the beginning it was difficult to say, but eventually I learned it. I feel totally different now that I know the meaning of the words. The words of the prayer are so powerful, saying that God is so powerful. You're busy praising Him and not feeling sorry for yourself. Kaddish doesn't allow for wallowing.

Kaddish brings peace.

Now memories make me feel close to my father. When I say Kaddish I feel close to him. But I don't always feel deeply connected.

I don't know if I believe in another world. When I pray I try and see if I can feel or touch God. Sometimes there's a glimmer of light. I am so scared of death, I shy away from thinking of it. There is no proof of Heaven.

On my father's yahrtzeit I feel better than I used to—not as pained. I light a candle and go to evening service. In his memory I gave money to an Israeli soldier's welfare fund as a special dedication.

There were things that my father did in life that I was ashamed of, and I should have been more forgiving. I have put it behind now, forgiving him in memory.

I never visit the cemetery. I can't bear the thought of looking at his grave without a stone. I fell into financial hardship and was divorced soon after his death, so his grave remains unmarked.

My relationship with God did change after losing my father. I started to pray more frequently. I wasn't used to praying every day in a formal fashion. I always feel more peaceful when I sit in synagogue and pray—always. You leave your common everyday nonsense behind you.

Every Friday night in *shul* I pray to be a better mother and person than last week. Sometimes that prayer is answered.

Arlene, twenty-nine, marketing executive
Lost her mother to a sudden heart attack after a long bout with another illness

My brother called to tell me our mother was dead. I just remember screaming for my husband. I was pregnant and thought for sure I would lose the baby. I thought that as long as I stood still this wouldn't be real.

I remember immediately giving my daughter "cheesies" to eat so that she would be quiet and happy. Rabbis and friends came over and were just there. People were around and created a very caring environment. I knew I wasn't alone.

I remember driving to the funeral and watching another funeral party get into a car accident. I was overwhelmed at the number of people who were there. The family was in the room waiting to go out to the service, and I felt a profound loss: this was it.

The rabbi spoke beautifully and said that God had plucked a flower from His garden. Mom would have liked that. Someone read her poetry.

At the grave site, we had to wait a long time because there were streams of cars. Everyone put earth on the coffin. There were no politics. Everyone was unified.

The shiva was surreal. Those who were observant came at off-hours when they knew they could sit down and give us comfort. They knew what to do. It affected my brothers.

I hated when people I didn't know would say, "Tell me about your mother." No, I didn't want to.

I did like it when people would talk about their own experiences of losing a parent. When you're going through it, it seems so hopeless, and to see someone who looks normal who has gone through it, it gives you hope.

A loss is something you never get over, but you learn to deal with it and integrate it into your life.

I give tzedakah to my mother's causes and feel she is still a part of my life, and I can continue on in her memory.

I didn't say Kaddish and felt it strange to be devoid of the obligation. At Yizkor after the first year, I was bawling, overwhelmed by all the emotions associated with a man saying Kaddish.

At her yahrtzeit I go to her grave site, and a Torah lecture is held in her honor. I don't feel more connected on her yahrtzeit because I never feel disconnected. To me the anniversary of her death is just marking time. Two years, three years—the loss is felt deeply all the time. I try and honor her memory all the time. The baby I was carrying when she died is named for her.

Her unveiling was nice. It was with close friends and family who really knew her and missed her. Once the marker is up, it feels real. It was hard deciding what to put on it—what people will see in 200 years—the color, the words.

The hardest time now is when I ask my kids who is in a picture and they don't know who she is. My oldest has a memory, and I show her pictures of her being held by my mother, but the baby never knew her, never will know her. That's the biggest loss. My kids will never get to know her and feel her warmth.

My relationship with God hasn't changed. I wasn't mad; I understood that He took her because her suffering was so great. It was her time. We were blessed with the time we had her.

Olam Habah? If I didn't believe in that, her death would be abhorrent. I know she went straight to Heaven.

I regret that the last time I saw her I didn't get a chance to say good night to her. Was I nice enough to her? Did I honor her enough? Did she know how much she meant to me? Now I can't increase those expressions or make our relationship better.

When I gave birth, I felt her presence. I felt her all around, her love and caring. When we knew the baby was a girl, I told my husband not to wait, to name her in *shul* the next morning for my mother.

Sharon, thirty-two, community worker
Lost her grandmother two years ago

My grandmother was the coolest lady I had ever known—she was way ahead of her time. I once asked her about her teenage years so many years ago, and she told me how she and her girlfriends secretly learned how to smoke cigarettes. She painted such a vivid scene of these proper "old-fashioned" girls behind the big house lighting up.

"How did you know what to do?" I asked.

"Honey, you just take a puff and let her go," she said with a twinkle in her eye.

Years later she lay dying in a home in Florida. My mother and sister were with her, but I couldn't travel, having just had a baby. It killed me not to be there, I was so close with her. She had been so sick, but somehow she was hanging on.

My mother called me on my car phone to update me, and she put the phone by my grandmother's ear, even though she wasn't conscious, so I could tell her that I loved her. I was driving and crying—I don't know how I did it.

Then she gave the phone to my sister, who told me that our grandmother was suffering but my sister thought she just wouldn't give herself permission to go. I begged my sister to give the phone back to Mom.

"Mom," I said, "You must tell Grandma something for me. Please, tell her, 'Take a puff and let her go.'"

My mom did not know what I was saying, but I begged her. I heard her bend down and tell her those exact words. There was a pause.

"Mom, mom!" I yelled.

My mother got back on the phone crying. "She's gone," she said. "She's gone."

Florence, sixty-two, homemaker
Lost her mother after a long illness to cancer

Every shiva is different. For me it was a different kind of mourning because my mother had had such a long and drawn-out illness. I had already mourned so much—mourned the loss of her legs, her mind. The shiva was a relief in that way. Now I could properly mourn the loss of her spirit and embrace the memories.

Michael, fifty-one, musician
Lost his father seven years ago after a massive heart attack; he was seventy-eight

For legal reasons, I hadn't been able to go back to Israel in over twenty years. Finally I was able to take my two kids and make the journey "home." It was wonderful to see my parents, and for the first week together it was clear that my father was having one of the best weeks of his life. He made a point of bringing us shopping, wanting to buy us all a special present. I have a picture of him that was taken during that week. We were in the market in Tel Aviv, and he was glowing.

My first night back, my father sat me down and asked me why my wife and I had separated. He didn't really listen to me; he just spoke. That was his way.

But a few days later we talked again, and to my amazement he was listening. I think it was for the first time. It meant so much to me that at last he was hearing me. We hugged and kissed and said good night. Seven hours later he was dead in my arms.

I had woken up and had just finished getting dressed when I heard my mother call out to me. My father had had a massive heart attack. I held him in my arms, feeling panic for about ten seconds. But then I relaxed. I knew this was it. And for some reason I felt at peace.

A few years back I had seen someone die, and he'd had the same look. I think I pounded on my father's chest. I don't remember. My most vivid

192

memory is simply holding him and saying, "It's okay. I'm here. It's okay." And then the ambulance came.

They worked on him for quite a while, but their efforts were futile. My father was gone. My mother went crazy.

My kids, who were nineteen and seventeen, were amazing. They were so supportive of my mother and me. I think my daughter held her grand-mother's hand twenty-four hours a day.

That week I found out that death is part of life. It's funny how we try and separate the two. When I was growing up, death was a bad word. My mother had been in the Holocaust, and death was filled with terror as if it didn't belong to us.

A few hours after my father died I remembered myself at age seven, when I couldn't imagine life without my dad. And here I was with my own kids and it all made sense.

I really tried to change this concept of death with my kids. When their hamster died, we buried it in the backyard and they saw that it was all part of life. Now that they were grown and were with me at this time, they under-stood, and we became even closer.

My strongest memory of the funeral is when they were lowering Dad into the grave. My mom was crying, and I was moved. I looked back and saw my oldest son beside my mother, holding her up. He was this big strong North American boy who didn't ever show his emotions. But at that moment his cheeks were wet.

I always thought of shiva as a circus, but we sat anyway. I did it for my mom. I wasn't devastated; there was a feeling of life. He lived, and now . . . I don't know where he is. I believe that a person's energy does not die. Call it a soul; it's just semantics. Whatever it is, I know that a part of him is somewhere.

I remember seeing my dad for the last time after the ambulance left and we were waiting for the burial society to come. I lifted up the blanket, and it was not my dad anymore.

We had had our troubled times together, but I loved his wonderful sense of childlike joy. When he was happy—at a wedding, a family get-together— he was happy like a child.

My sister didn't handle it well—his death, I mean. She had unfinished business with him that was never resolved. She had a harder time with it than I did.

I went to the cemetery once since then, with my mom. I don't believe my dad is there in the ground, but my mom does. She was so sweet, she was talking to him while we were there and telling him I had come.

She goes every year on his yahrtzeit. I myself do nothing to mark it. While I was in Israel for the week of shiva, I said Kaddish, but I didn't relate to it at all. I feel I can communicate with my father in my own way.

Sometimes I find myself thinking of him and the things he passed on to me—half of his genes, a lot of his temper, some of his joy. The older I get the more I look like him. It's scary.

It didn't hit me until a month after his death that something within him knew that he would die. Why would he be so insistent to buy us each a special gift? Why would he listen to me for the first time in years? Why was it this week, the first time I had returned in twenty years? He could have died the week before or the week after.

I read somewhere that in China they have a week in which everyone honors old people. It was found that the mortality rate significantly lowers the week before and during that week. Afterward the mortality rate goes up again.

He hadn't been well, but he knew I was coming. My mother feels that he held on for me. I think she is right.

Rhonda, thirty-five, hotel manager
Lost a beloved teacher nine years ago to AIDS

I was in college and this teacher was a pivotal person in my life whose way of teaching changed me forever and connected me to God in a way I had never been before.

He was my dance teacher. He wasn't Jewish, but he was extremely connected, very spiritual. He taught dance as life: being present, honoring the journey, not worrying about the result of how things work, being real, having courage. He taught strength, and he taught vulnerability. He was very gifted.

Most people like that don't know how much they affect other people, but years later I made a point of letting him know. He was very moved.

Because of him I learned a way of accessing a journey and made a decision to pursue dance professionally. It was a life decision based on what I saw possible from his teaching.

I went to New Mexico and was with a dance company there. I brought him there to give workshops, and two years later he moved there too. He was gay. I think he knew even then that he was HIV positive and didn't have long to live.

I started to take classes from him again. I suspected he was sick. I made a point of giving him a lot of positive feedback so he could see his goodness. We talked a lot about spiritual issues. I was growing Jewishly at the time and he was very interested.

I made a decision to go to Israel, and he asked me to dance in his company. I never followed up; I got too busy. Then I decided not to go after all, but I never told him that I didn't leave.

One day I got an impulse to go visit him at his house, but for some reason I didn't go. A few days later, I found out that was the day he had died. The circumstances were mysterious.

I never saw him really sick, but I heard it was horrific. I feel I should have been there for him; I regret that. I haven't come to terms with it.

There was no funeral. I went to the memorial service and spoke. I shared the impact he had on my life. It was very healing.

I think of him now whenever I think about dance. When I think of my life as a journey, I think of him encouraging me in that way. Listening to my spiritual instincts inside—that's what I learned from him.

I haven't danced since he died. He was unique. I knew I would never find another teacher like him again.

He wouldn't be upset that I stopped dancing. He didn't care if I danced, as long as I was fully doing what I was supposed to be doing and was being "present"—being in reality, not in illusion.

He would be happy with my life now, and my dedication to Judaism.

For the first couple of years, I wrote about him, memories and reflections on his teachings, things I would have wanted to tell him. On the anniversary of his death, I would call out his name, as people would recognize yahrtzeits.

If someone asks me who had a powerful impact on my life, I always mention him. I can still picture him now in class, coming up to me and asking, "Where are you?" "Are you present?" "Wake up."

I believe in another world. He is there. And he is present.

Linda, thirty-seven, teacher
Lost her grandmother to cancer twenty years ago

She was my favorite grandmother because she knew what kids liked. Our greatest treat was sleeping over at her house. She lived in an apartment building, and we loved riding up and down the elevators pretending we were secret spies, following people and playing imaginary games.

She was from the old country and spoke with a heavy accent, but she was the coolest grandmother ever. She brought us to bingo games and hosted poker parties in her home. She bought us comic books and let us stay up late watching movies. Breakfast was always pastry or donuts. We could sleep in as late as we wanted, but we had too much fun to waste our time there sleeping.

She made us fried *matzah* even if it wasn't Passover. And she let us suck on sugar cubes from our grandfather's sugar jar.

I remember when my mom told me that my grandmother was sick. It sounded like nothing, that she just wasn't feeling well, but soon she was in the hospital.

I went to visit her, but she didn't look like her. She looked small and all the bubbling energy was gone. My heart raced. She was dying.

It was only a few weeks later that we were called by the hospital. It was near the end. We all came and gathered around her bed. All the grandchildren took turns holding her hand. She was on life support at this point and didn't even know we were there.

When it was my turn to be with her, I remember holding her hand and looking out the hospital window at the street below. I was struck by how normal the world looked out there. Here I was experiencing the death of someone I loved for the very first time, and people were out there eating, driving, talking, laughing. How could it be?

We were all there when she finally died. They took the oxygen mask off her, and my mom went in to see her for the last time. I looked in. She didn't look like my grandmother at all. I wish I hadn't seen her like that. I wanted only to remember her as she was, full of life, yelling at my grandfather, slipping us dollars for the candy store, and planning her next poker game.

And now she was gone.

I have no memories of the funeral or the shiva. And when I go to her grave I don't feel connected at all. The times I feel close to her are life-affirming moments—at family *simchas*, the namings of my children, and graduations.

I wanted my first baby to be a girl so I could name her after my grandmother. During my pregnancy I had a dream that she would be a girl and that she would bear her name. She was, and she does. It is bittersweet, for I wish my daughter were named for someone else and had her great-grandmother here to love instead.

But it wasn't meant to be. I miss her so much.

Marsha, fifty, writer
Lost her father seventeen years ago; he was sixty-two

My parents lived far away. I knew my father had been sick, but until I went to visit I didn't realize how sick. He didn't even recognize me. I was in shock.

They didn't know what it was, and the doctors knew it was serious but they hid it from us. He was a vegetable within a few weeks. It was awful.

I was so naive. I should have demanded more information, but all the doctors said was just to sit with him. I didn't know what that meant. I didn't know it meant nothing could be done. My mother thought he'd be alright and she would take him home from the hospital and take care of him. He never came home.

We were all in denial, and the doctors fed on it. They robbed us of the time to prepare we would have had if we had known the truth.

I wasn't in touch then with the spiritual side of life, so when he was totally out of it no one stayed with him. My mother had to keep the store running, and I didn't realize that I should have been there talking to him. Even though he wasn't be able to answer, on a soul level he would have been comforted. I feel bad about that.

One morning my mother called and said he had passed away. My brother made all the funeral arrangements. My uncle flew in just in time to go straight to the cemetery for the funeral.

At the cemetery I was laughing and making jokes. My sister-in-law took me aside and told me she had been the same way after her father died. She told me I was being hysterical. She was right. I quickly gained my composure.

My thoughts: this really isn't happening; it's all a dream. I was in total disbelief. I didn't cry. I wanted to, but I didn't.

I remember thinking that I had no idea my father knew so many people. My uncle was lamenting in Yiddish in a loud voice. They did *kriah*, in which our clothes were torn. It was so unreal. After the shiva I left the clothes with my mother. I never wanted to wear those clothes again.

During the shiva we sat low and people brought food. My uncles came during the day but they didn't sleep over. It was strange to hear all the good things people had to say about my father and what he had done for them. I felt bitter. So much time for others but no time for me.

We went through his things, and I found all the letters and cards I had ever sent for the last fifteen years. He had kept them all, and he'd kept them so neat. I was very surprised. Why would he keep them? What I wrote was superficial—travel postcards, pictures of the kids—nothing deep or meaningful. I took all the letters and burned them. I had to do it. Now I feel guilty about it.

I also burned some philosophical writings of his that I found. I was angry. I felt this was the end and I wanted nothing left. I didn't know about spirit. I thought I was closing everything.

During that week Mom told me that she would talk to Dad on the balcony. I thought it was weird, but I told her to keep doing it.

It's funny; I thought my mother was the most important person in my life, but he was the one who always wrote me and kept me connected.

When I got back home, I would find myself feeling this light and love, and I knew it was my father. His death brought me in touch with my own mortality. I didn't take my life seriously until then; now I started taking more control.

I began to learn about spirit and the next world. It was a turning point in my life. Up until then, it had been all material and physical, and now there was more.

I don't mark his yahrtzeit in any way because I don't know what I should be doing on that day. I'd like to know more about it. Because he is buried so far away, I don't go to his grave site. My mother goes regularly with my brother. Even when I go back, I don't go to his grave; it's just a stone. If his soul wanted to hover anywhere, it wouldn't be there, it would be in Jerusalem, for he was a very devout man.

His whole death for me was like being in a car accident and getting whiplash or something. It snapped me out of my life, and suddenly I knew what was real. But it's a journey, and it's taking a long time.

I feel my growing observance now is being guided, as if he is blessing this slow return. He tried to raise us religiously, but we rebelled against the formality of it all. He wants me now to have the joy of Judaism that he had a hard time transferring. My father was only happy on Shabbat, but even then he couldn't share his happiness.

I didn't take anything of my father's back with me after his death; I didn't want anything. But I did ask for his candlesticks. They are stored away right now. I'm not ready to use them yet. Perhaps soon I will.

As part of my spiritual journey, I want to go to Israel to study. I inherited some jewelry from my father that he had bought from people just because they needed money. The jewelry didn't mean anything to him, nor does it mean anything to me. So I have decided to sell it to finance a learning trip to Jerusalem in a few weeks.

I am going back to Israel to learn. I know he is with me, and I know he is pleased.

Jake, forty-six, medical technician
His twenty-one-year-old daughter was killed in Iraq three months ago

Inspired by the events of September 11, two years ago my daughter, Catherine, joined the air force. Three months ago a captain and a chaplain in service dress came to my door at seven in the morning. They didn't have to say anything. I knew my beautiful daughter was dead.

I have a military background, having served in the Navy years ago, but I wasn't overjoyed when she told me she was joining up. I am not antiservice, but I didn't feel her personality was highly suited for a long stint in the military. I wasn't happy, but she was determined, so I supported her.

She trained in Texas and enjoyed the military. This past June she was shipped out to Iraq. I traveled to Texas to say good-bye. I have only told my wife this, but somewhere inside I knew I would never see her again.

Catherine's mother is not Jewish. We were divorced in 1987, but I stayed close with Catherine and her sister and saw them every other week. Recently, Catherine became very interested in the Jewish side of her heritage. I had become religious in the past few years and had remarried. She was so interested that she insisted on putting "Jewish" on her dog tags, even though it could possibly have caused more harm to her over there.

I asked her why she did that, and she said, "I just felt it was the right thing to do."

Catherine felt that she was not only protecting America by fighting but she was also protecting the State of Israel.

I couldn't speak to the captain and chaplain who came to my door that morning, so it was my wife who got all of the details. Apparently Catherine was in the lead vehicle of a convoy, providing security. Her vehicle was struck by a roadside bomb. A sergeant in the army was also killed. He left behind a wife and kids.

It took ten days for them to fly her remains back to the States. From Iraq to Kuwait to Germany to Delaware and finally to Florida, where she was to be buried. Jewish law encourages a quick burial, so it was painful to have such a long time pass.

I had to identify her remains. The bomb had ripped her apart.

The fact that she had insisted on putting "Jewish" on her dog tags gave me the ability to prevent embalming and other things that were against Jewish law. I was able to choose a plain wood casket. Her mother, although not

Jewish, went along with anything I wanted done. She was relieved not to have to make any decisions.

There was a memorial service for her before the burial, and I spoke. A lot of press members were there and at the graveside. Unfortunately, much of the press wants to exploit the pain of the families of fallen servicemen and servicewomen to bolster antiwar sentiment. I did not want to be their tool, so I was not able to fully express my grief at the funeral.

After the burial we went to a room near the site of the funeral where there were food and drinks. A lot of the military were there, hot in full dress, and that was the only real shiva I had. I sat and people came and spoke to me and tried to give me comfort.

I am still mourning—not publicly, but my thoughts often turn to her. She was an outgoing ray of sunshine, and I feel blessed to have known her for as long as I did. She was a real fireball and always honored me. They sent me her possessions. Her cell phone was filled with calls to me, calls received from me, and messages from me that were saved.

When the captain and the chaplain came to the door, I was in the middle of learning Torah. After they left, I went back to learning, this time in her memory. The experience of losing her has made me a more deeply religious person. I had progressed religiously, but my connection to faith, love, and awe of God on an emotional level had never sparked. What happened to Catherine gave me that.

I have worked in the medical field for years and have seen a lot of kids die. My daughter did not die because of drugs or some car accident or suicide. I take solace knowing that she died doing something bigger than herself—protecting and defending the United States and Israel.

Although I am still angry at those who killed her, I am at peace with her circumstances. She didn't suffer. And she is my hero.

Anna, thirty-five, marketing director
Lost her mother eleven years ago to a heart attack brought on by diabetes;
she was sixty-two

I don't remember who called me to tell me the news. Was it my father? I really don't remember. All I remember is collapsing in the kitchen. I was three months pregnant. My mother was dead.

She was the quiet strength in my life, overflowing with creativity, energy, warmth, and caring. She had been sick my whole life, but I could tell her anything.

My mother battled diabetes, which put her in and out of the hospital for as long as I could remember. One of my earliest memories was being three and standing on the kitchen counter reaching for something my mother wanted and couldn't reach because she was confined to a wheelchair.

Why did I collapse? I guess it was from shock, though my brothers and I knew my mother would not live to old age. We were always mentally prepared, but when the time finally came, I was overwhelmed.

The funeral was surreal. I remember discussing the plans, rabbis coming over to help. I remember something the rabbi said that really touched me. He talked about a gardener picking a flower from the garden and bringing it home. Clearly that was what God was doing with my mother.

The first thud of earth on the coffin is the hardest thing to hear in the world. It echoes its finality. It signals that there is no going back; it's really not a mistake. It's over. And the reality means my life has to go on without her.

The shiva was overwhelming. I was the only one who really sat, as I was the only one in the family who had become observant. So many people came, some to give comfort, some just to be seen. It was far too public.

I remember a stranger sitting down in front of me at our shiva and saying, "Tell me something fabulous about your mother." All I thought was, I don't know you. I should tell a stranger something fabulous about my mother? Someone else said, "When your dad is ready, I have a great girl for him." And someone chastised me for being alone in the study when someone was looking for me. What—am I on display?

Today I don't go to the shiva house unless I am very close with the person; otherwise, I send a note or make a donation.

The best shiva call was when a friend came and brought cookies baked by her daughter for me. She just sat and gave them with such a full heart. The rest of the shiva was kind of like a zoo.

I miss my mother. I miss her counsel. I often think how my life would be different if she were alive. She was the quiet voice of reason and peace in the family. She was the one who kept it all together. My daughter is so much like me; I wish my mother were here to give me wisdom so I could raise her properly.

I rarely go to her grave site. I don't feel that it is the only place I can talk to her. I find being there makes me remember her with sadness. I find it foreign. I want to remember her with joy.

The baby I was carrying when she died carries her name. And she is very much like her: artistic, loves little kids, unconcerned about material things, reads people's souls.

"They" say the loss gets easier with time, and in some ways that's true. For the first few months, I would just spontaneously cry. You think the pain will never go away, but it does. Then you miss the tears because you realize that you have moved on.

I look at her picture every day, but every day I get further and further away from remembering her voice.

Mourning is so private, but you have to put the mourning in its place, and living the best life you can, in the end, is the best way to honor someone's memory.

Lisa, forty-five, writer

Lost her father-in-law to respiratory arrest five months ago

I loved my father-in-law, and I know he loved me. How did I know? Every time I would call him, he would say a regular "Hello," and then when he realized it was me, his voice would jump in a loving, animated way and he would give me the warmest and most enthusiastic "Hello, Lisa!"

He suffered from poor health his whole life and almost died as a child, but he had the greatest sense of humor and outlook on life. Perhaps because of his childhood illness, he looked at things differently, appreciated life more than the average person.

He was the consummate Zaidy (grandfather), throwing in Yiddish words when he spoke, a throwback to the old country grandparents even though he was American born. Whenever he would visit, he would spend the hours when the kids were in school reading *Yiddish Proverbs*, a book we had around the house.

He was a schmoozer and could talk for hours, even if you didn't talk back. Everything in life was interesting to him, and he always managed to see the funny side of everything, be it politics, sports, systems, or people. And boy, did he love his grandchildren.

He could sit with them forever, talking, drawing (he was quite the accomplished artist), and just enjoying them. They called him "Chicago Zaidy," as opposed to their other Zaidy, who was just "Zaidy." He loved that. Before my kids were born, his other grandchildren called him Grandpa, but since I grew up with grandfathers called Zaidy, I couldn't bring myself to have them call him Grandpa. It just didn't sound Jewish. And he loved the "Chicago Zaidy" moniker because he was so, so Jewish.

For most of his life, he wasn't Jewish in the religious sense, more with the cultural trappings—Yiddish, blintzes, bagels, lox—but his son, my husband, became religious as a young adult, and after many years, it started to rub off.

In the last years of his life, he started to pray. First it was informal and spontaneous, and then my husband got him a *siddur* (prayer book) with English translation and transliteration, and he began to *daven* (pray) every day. He always told me that he didn't think he had a right to pray since he was such a sinner. He didn't mean that he had robbed or murdered, but he had deep regrets that he hadn't lived a more observant life. But I think he came to realize that even if someone made a lifetime of mistakes, it's never too late.

We arranged for him to have a learning partner over the phone (in a wonderful program called Partners in Torah), and when it was time for our son's *bar mitzvah*, he insisted on buying him *tefillin*, along with the other Zaidy. When my husband went to pick up the *tefillin*, he decided to buy a set for his father too. He presented them to him and showed him how to use them. From that day on he put on *tefillin* every day.

Years before, my father-in-law had begun to wear a *yarmulke* (kippah, or skull-cap) around the house. That began when he traveled to us for the opening of the new synagogue where his son, my husband, was the rabbi. When we danced and sang the Torah scrolls from the old, storefront synagogue to the new, beautiful building, someone brought my father-in-law in under the *chuppah* to hold the scroll. It was too heavy for him, so my husband helped him. He turned away and said he couldn't do it because he wasn't wearing a *yarmulke*. A great rabbi who was there took off his black hat, removed his own *yarmulke* that was underneath, and handed it to my father-in-law.

At the end of the day, he went to give it back to the rabbi, but the rabbi told him to please keep it. He went home and every day wore that *yarmulke*.

When he was at the end of his life, in the hospital, he was distressed. Why? Because when the paramedics had taken him from home to the hospital, he forgot to take his *yarmulke*. My sister-in-law went back to his place and searched until she found it, brought it to the hospital, and placed it on his head. It gave him peace.

My father-in-law was the first of our parents to pass away. Although we all know it will happen one day, we live in denial and are shocked when it happens. Someone once told me when I was dating that I should keep in mind that whomever I marry will be the person who will one day get me through the loss of my parents. That woke me up to looking for someone with depth, compassion, sensitivity, and wisdom. Before that, dating was about being cute and having fun.

I wanted to support my husband and prayed that I would somehow have the right words and strength to help him through his father's death. I encouraged him to fly home frequently to see his father when he fell ill and to be there for his mother and sisters. Sometimes he hesitated to go, thinking his father had taken a turn for the better. But I would book the ticket anyway so he would go. Later he deeply thanked me, for, in the end, his father had much less time than anyone thought, and those last days were so precious.

The last night of my father-in-law's life, my husband was with him in the hospital. Before he left, he said Shema with him (See question 6 of "The Ten Most Commonly Asked Questions about Death" in section 4), which is supposed to be the last thing you say before you go to sleep and the last thing on your lips before you die. My father-in-law only knew it in English, but he remembered every word.

I flew in with two of our kids for the funeral. My oldest daughter, who was away at school, had flown in a couple of weeks before he died to spend time with him, so she didn't come in for the funeral. She was graduating in a few days.

The funeral was surreal. My husband spoke of his father. He said that he loved his father very much. He used to call him every day, not to make his father happy (though he knew it did) but to make himself happy. He enjoyed talking to his dad, and that daily call was a daily pleasure, not a burden or obligation.

The shiva was challenging as most of the men who came did not know how to pray properly, but my husband had to say Kaddish, so he helped them and everyone did their best. He traveled back home in the middle of the week to finish sitting shiva in his own home. He arrived very late at night. I wasn't there as I had to attend our daughter's graduation. But I called a friend and asked if he could arrange for ten men to be in our home, even though it was late, so that my husband could say Kaddish.

My husband did not expect this to happen as he was arriving very late. But word had spread, and when he arrived, the house was overflowing with people—men and women who came to comfort him and make sure he could say Kaddish. It was an incredible out-pouring of love. I felt so proud to be part of the Jewish people.

He is still in the first year of mourning, and I try very hard to make sure he is able to get to *shul* to say Kaddish every day, even if it means going that extra mile, covering kids' carpools and rescheduling my appointments. I know how important it is to him, and I do everything I can to help make it happen.

Because he sometimes has to travel to places where there is no place to say Kaddish, he arranged for Kaddish to be said three times every day for the first year in Jerusalem. He gave money to sponsor a rabbinic student in his studies there, and that student makes sure Kaddish is said for my father-in-law. So if for some reason my husband is unable to do it, he is comforted in knowing that in Israel it is being done on his behalf. (See question 8 of "The Ten Most Commonly Asked Questions about Death" in section 4.)

I really don't know how my husband feels this year, and he doesn't talk about it much. Occasionally he will say how much he misses his father. The unveiling is coming up in a few months, and we will travel for the ceremony. I wonder if that will bring some sort of closure, but I doubt it. Someone else who lost his parents told me you are never really the same after that. I guess that is why, when you tear your garment at the funeral, for a parent it is done on the left side, over the heart. For any other loss, the tear is made over the right side.

For our parents gave us life. And when they die, a part of us, living deep in our hearts, is gone forever.

As a daughter-in-law, the whole process was very difficult for me. I was so busy being supportive of my husband, handling everything at home when he was away, being there for my kids, traveling from the funeral to our daughter's graduation alone, taking care of the house and my husband's needs during shiva, I never had a chance to mourn my father-in-law.

One night, weeks after the shiva, I went into the car in the driveway and sat there alone and cried and cried. It felt good to let it out. No structure of mourning is provided for an in-law. The customs are all focused on the immediate family, but I was in pain too.

When I think of him, I have wonderful memories, but there is a lingering sadness that is not going away. Perhaps with time.

Sheri, fifty-one, party planner
Lost her father to cancer nine months ago and her mother three years ago

I am a convert to Judaism, so the loss of a parent who is not Jewish posed a challenge for me. My parents were special, and I loved them deeply. When I told them that I was studying Judaism and planned to convert and marry a Jewish man, they were incredibly supportive.

Judaism has a wise and supportive system for comforting mourners, but that is only when one loses a Jewish loved one. A Jew does not sit shiva for a non-Jew.

So what was I to do? There was so much to deal with. Not only dealing with the loss of each of my parents but having to cope with non-Jewish siblings, priests, churches, crosses and cemeteries! It was a mourning minefield.

I know I should have asked our rabbi what I was allowed to do and not do, but I just couldn't. So I decided for myself, based on my family situation, what I was going to do. I went to the church, the burial, and accepted the priest (who, in the case of my mother's death, ironically turned out to be a lapsed Jew).

But it was the after-funeral situation that was my biggest hurdle. My siblings went back to their cities and lives, and I returned to my city. I knew sitting shiva was inappropriate, and my Jewish friends and community knew that too, so what was I to do?

The first time, when I lost my mother, I just sat around the house and felt sorry for myself. So when I lost my father I made it clear to my friends that, even though I was not formally sitting shiva, I would very much appreciate it if they would call and come by. Those calls and visits meant so much to me.

No Kaddish is said for people who are not Jewish, so I decided to invent my own daily way of remembering my parents and elevating their souls. For my mother I took pictures of flowers, because she loved nature so much, and put them together in an album in her memory. I also donated money to the local horticultural society to have a bench placed in their floral gardens with a plaque in her memory.

I go there often, sit, and think of my mother. I also like to go and take pictures of children sitting and standing on the bench. I know she is smiling down from heaven and getting pleasure from the fact that they are laughing and playing on her bench.

For my father I donated money to a foundation that educates people about herbs and alternative medicines because that is something he felt passionately about. I then decided to learn Torah in his memory. So every day I learn a little bit, and I have in mind that the wisdom that is strengthening me is elevating him.

I would tell someone who is a convert to Judaism to prepare their friends to help you through the awkwardness of the non-shiva mourning. They really don't know what to do, so you have to guide them. They want to be there for you.

David, forty-two, advertising executive
Lost a friend in high school to a car accident

I had just graduated from high school, and it was the summer before college. My friends and I were on such a high—our whole lives were ahead of us.

I remember coming home, and my mother told me that one of my friends had called and that there had been some sort of accident involving another friend. My heart stopped. My head flooded with thoughts of my best friends, and the idea that one of them might be hurt was just horrifying.

I called and found out the news. One of my friends, who had taken a summer job in Vancouver (we lived in Toronto), was killed in a car accident on his way out there. His girlfriend and her friend were also killed.

How could it be? How could it be that someone so young, someone I knew, was dead?

He was one of only a handful of Jews at our school. So the gang looked to me, not knowing what was appropriate to do at a Jewish funeral and something called the shiva. At the time I was Jewish but didn't know much about it. I had memorized something for my *bar mitzvah*, gotten up and recited it, had no idea what I was saying or what it meant, and enjoyed the party and all the gifts. Dreidels on Chanukah and *matzah* on Passover were about the extent of my Jewish knowledge. If you had asked me back then, I would have said that I was an atheist because that was what my mother was.

I was one of the few of our social group who had my own car, so I offered to drive a bunch of them to the funeral, which took place at a Jewish cemetery way out of town. My friends, who were not Jewish and many of whom were religious Christians, piled into the car, and off we went.

I remember standing at the graveside as the earth was going on to the casket, and at that moment I knew there was a God. I knew it like I knew I had five fingers on one hand. I turned to my best friend who was standing beside me and said to him, "There's a God." He went to church every Sunday. He turned to me and nodded.

I didn't tell anyone else my epiphany. I knew they would think that I wanted a God to exist because my friend was dead, that I needed God so it wasn't just "lights out." I knew that wasn't true, but I couldn't explain it. I just knew.

Did that change my life in any way? Not really. I was still on a very secular track: college, non-Jewish girlfriends, career . . . But it planted a seed.

Years later, when I was backpacking around the world, I ended up in Israel. It was a life-changing experience. The wisdom I heard and the people that I met there were the water I needed for that seed.

Something inside me began to grow, and the more that I learned, the more that it grew. Today I live a fully observant life, with God as the central theme.

I hope that a part of my life, and all the deep pleasures that have come from it, are somehow a tribute to my high school friend. I don't know why he had to die so young—perhaps so that I could truly live.

Alan, thirty-nine, editor
Lost his brother to encephalitis when he was a child

My brother died a week before my seventh birthday. He was five years old.

He had juvenile diabetes, which attacked his immune system; as a result he contracted herpes. Encephalitis put him into a coma for the last six months of his life.

I loved my brother. He was my best friend. My memories are sketchy, but I do remember nurses coming and showing my parents how to give him insulin injections, and when they did he always cried. Sometimes I would wake up in the middle of the night and sneak out of my room and see my parents standing over my brother's bed, speaking in hushed tones.

When he slipped into a coma, he was taken to a hospital about thirty minutes away. We visited him often, but he was unresponsive. I don't remember having any feelings during those visits, I just have an overall sterile-environment image that doesn't go away.

Eventually he was moved to a children's hospice, which was like a large home with a lot of cribs. No one moved in the cribs.

We would travel there, and my other brother and I would sit in the play-room with all of the toys while my parents went to my brother's room. I didn't know he was going to die.

They called to tell us he was near the end, and we were all at the hospice when he passed away. My mother came to the playroom and asked us if we wanted to say good-bye. My parents cried. We did not. But I knew we would never be coming back there again.

My parents were Jewish but very far from knowing what the Jewish thing to do was. The funeral was in our home, and I remember a lot of people being there. Mom asked us if we wanted to draw pictures and put them in the casket. The coffin was right there in our house. They took it away and cremated him, which I now know is forbidden in Judaism, and they buried the ashes on our property. There was no tombstone, but sometimes we would visit the spot where he was buried.

When my parents divorced, the house was sold and my brother's ashes were moved to a cemetery nearby. There is a tombstone now, but with no Jewish name on it.

It's hard for me to think about how it was all handled because now I am a much more knowledgeable and observant Jew, and I realize that it was not handled in the right way. But we didn't know. Most Jews don't.

There was no shiva, and every year on his birthday, my mother is very sad. I know she hasn't fully mourned him.

On the anniversary of his death, on the secular calendar, she lights a candle. No one says Kaddish. No one ever said Kaddish for my brother. Maybe now I should. I haven't asked those kinds of questions because it's all too painful.

On his yahrtzeit I light a candle. It's the same day as my grandfather's yahrtzeit.

I named my fourth daughter after him. I had held the name in case I had a son, but I was told that it was fine to name a girl after a boy. We just chose the feminine equivalent. It was powerful for my parents, and I know it made them happy when I gave her his name. I actually think it is better that I never had a boy. I think if he had exactly the same name as my brother, it would have been too much for all of us.

My other brother and I never talk about our brother dying. Dad doesn't talk about it. And I know it would be too difficult to talk to my mom. I guess that's not so healthy. Now that I am a father, I can more deeply appreciate the pain my parents must have gone through. It has made me a better son.

You would think that I would worry about my daughters and their health, but I don't. I think this is because, after becoming observant, I have learned that it's not really Jewish to worry. We are supposed to do our best; the rest is up to God.

That's a relief; otherwise I think it would occupy my whole life.

Jennifer, forty-five, homemaker
Lost her father last year to heart failure

I grew up in an abusive home, so when my father—the main source of the physical, sexual, and emotional abuse—died, I had very mixed feelings.

My father had an anger issue, and I had a very unhappy childhood because of it. I am working very hard at remaking myself as a happy adult, but the childhood was just awful.

My father drank and was just plain mean. But there was also another side to him. I know it's hard to understand, even for me, but we were a close family. When he was in his fifties, he got cancer and suffered a series of heart attacks. His weakened physical state meant we lived our family life around him.

214

My mother, who also suffered at the hand of my father, seemed indifferent to his illness. And she also did little to care for us. We ate dinner in front of the television, never as a family around the table.

He died in his seventies. The last two years of his life were not pretty. His mind was breaking down, which only made his temper worse, and then his body quickly followed. He was never hospitalized, and he was home until the end.

Since high school I have chosen a road of healing through counseling. My family would never go, but for me it was a priority. In my early thirties I told my father I was unhappy and I didn't know how to live my life. I knew he loved me but was incapable of seeing how much he hurt me.

I married and started my own family.

When my father became ill, I flew back on a regular basis to see him. I was able to actually laugh with him. I tried to talk with him about the abuse, but he seemed to have no memory of it. I kept flying back during the last weeks. Why? I think I had reached a point where I accepted my parents for who they were, even with all of their failings.

But the last time I saw him, I couldn't kiss him good-bye. There was too much past, too many painful memories.

I was home when I got the call that my father had died. I had no emotion and did not shed a tear. My friends helped me pack, and I traveled to the funeral. The synagogue was packed, and I gave the eulogy. My sisters all flew in and were there. Yes, we were abused, but here we were, alive and actually close. And, though neglected, we all knew that our father had loved us.

The shiva was packed; people came and shared the nice side of my father with us. He had been very devoted to his father and his mother-in-law. He had a lot of friends. It was hard to hear nice things. I responded intellectually and thanked them for sharing.

The death, the funeral, the shiva—I just didn't connect to any of it. I suppose I was in shock. The only emotion I felt was relief. He was dead.

It's all so complicated. My father gave me life, we traveled, and he sent me to college and graduate school. He loved me, but I can't say that I loved him. I don't even know what that means.

We just had the unveiling. The rabbi spoke and said that my father was a complicated man. Poems and prayers were said.

I do regret that I never told him I loved him. Even if you don't feel it at the moment, you should say it, because no matter what they have done, you still really do love them. It's not good to have regrets, even if it is complicated.

Faith, thirty-nine, fashion buyer
Lost her husband suddenly to cancer three years ago

I was with him when my husband stopped breathing. I was numb. Only a week before he had complained of not feeling well and went in for tests. I'm not religious, but my first thought was, when would I see him again? In the Next World? I had such a strong sense that his soul was still there and wondered how long it would take to leave his body. I remember being upset that my two little girls weren't there.

I was in shock, disbelief. I left the room and forced myself to focus. How was I going to explain it to the girls? I don't remember how I got home. Did I go for a walk?

Somehow I found myself inside my home and I told them the truth. I told them his body wasn't working any more, but his soul was still alive and will always be. My seven-year-old cried and ran to her room angry and slammed the door. My five-year-old didn't understand.

At the funeral service I remember only a few things—the eternal flame burning, the rabbi talking about my husband. The rabbi was a friend of ours and said things I didn't even know about him. He himself started crying.

I was stunned. I couldn't believe I was looking at a coffin that had his body in it. I was in denial. I had made the decision that I wanted the girls to be there, so I had to keep myself together for them. I remember wondering what he looked like and wanting to touch him.

At the burial his mother totally broke down. I was worried she would die with him. I didn't know how I would stand up as I saw the coffin being lowered into the grave. The feeling—I can't even put it into words. It was more a physical sensation—surreal. I felt superimposed upon it, as I were watching it from the outside.

I think I spoke at the graveside. I didn't want it to end. I wanted to share little bits and pieces with everyone—his smile and how much he loved people. I wanted them to remember him at his best. I couldn't believe it was happening, that I was there for that purpose. I was very concerned for my kids.

He was buried beside my grandparents, and I remember thinking he would be happy. He admired them and wanted to emulate my grandfather.

I wasn't prepared for the service at the grave site. It wasn't spiritual for me. It was too painful. The pain, the ache—it was so physical.

Kaddish, shiva—I had never understood them. I thought they were a curiosity of the religion. But at this time I had the benefit of people explaining them to me. Judaism is brilliant. I never even believed in God until after he died, and now I was reaffirming my belief. I felt so close to God, and it was a tremendous comfort, but it took time. My relationship with God completely changed. It was a beautiful outgrowth from a tragic situation.

I walked through the shiva, but I was there only in body. People said the strangest things—"You'll feel better in time." It's true, but you don't want to hear that. "Why haven't you called me?" said another! "You're going to be fine." You're not fine! The worst part was when people would come up to me and look grief stricken and say, "How are you?" I also didn't like being told that I was young and I could start a new life. And, because he suffered, they would say that at least he was out of his pain now. No, I didn't like that. When someone dies that you love, you don't want him dead under any circumstances.

I liked it more when they would say that they were thinking of me and they were here for me. The less said the better. I didn't like positive remarks. The best part was when they just sat. That told me, "I'm here for you. If you want me, I'm here."

The prayers meant a lot, and people coming for the services at the shiva was meaningful. It was hard to sit in a chair for seven days. Then it made sense to me. Originally my family was going to make the shiva four days. We thought, let's not feel it, let's put it behind us. But my teacher explained that sitting for seven days was important, that I needed to feel it, resolve it, and then let it go.

I struggled reading Hebrew, and I went to *shul* for the shloshim. My husband's death was the beginning of my belief. Otherwise his death made no sense.

All the customs are so brilliant. I felt as though I was in a cocoon and then slowly going into the world to become a normal, functioning person.

I was very fortunate that I had a special Jewish teacher in my life to help me through all of it. I thank God that she was in my life.

My feelings on my husband's yahrtzeit are different now than during the first year. His death is still hard for me to accept, but the yahrtzeit isn't a huge, horrible day like it was. I have very mixed feelings. I think about my kids. I remember the good. I feel lonely for him. I take the girls to the cemetery. We paint rocks, write letters, send them up in balloons—every year it's something different. It changes with time.

When I'm at the cemetery, that's as close as I can get to him. I feel his soul. I feel closer to him. In the silence I have private thoughts. It's a "we" experience. I go on our anniversary and experience it.

I go to the synagogue and say Kaddish. It's comforting. It's a time to remember and focus. We light a candle and give tzedakah.

The first six months I couldn't talk or think straight. We made a "Daddy Box" where the kids could write poems and put them in. I still write in a diary, something to him.

The unveiling was a more positive experience. We were very prepared, and the girls and I talked about how we wanted it to be so he could be remembered in a happy way. We brought stones from our house and the girls passed them out for everyone to put on his stone. I felt he was there and smiling, happy.

Yizkor makes me feel sad, and I miss him, but I've come to realize that death is a part of life. He's not with me, but he always has a presence. I do believe in another world, in Olam Habah. Yes I do. I always wish he were here, but I never feel far away.

Remembering

Always

The next four pages can be used to record special memories you have. Perhaps paste a few pictures, notes, or a memento in the space below. You might want to record your feelings of loss or your experience of mourning.

In a Jewish House of Mourning

Each culture approaches death and the mourning period in its own unique fashion. As a family, we deeply appreciate your coming to our home to offer your support and comfort. We request that an effort be made to focus conversation on the life and legacy of the departed. Painful as it may seem, attempts at distracting family members from thinking or speaking about their loss are not considered appropriate at this time. Again, thank you for coming. Your very presence here brings us great comfort and is appreciated more than you will ever know.

From *Remember My Soul*, by Lori Palatnik with Rabbi Yaakov Palatnik, K'hal Publishing, 2008.

Notes

SECTION ONE

1. Maimonides, "Hilchot Teshuvah" [Laws of Repentance], in Mishneh Torah, vol. 1, *Madda* [Knowledge], chap. 8, law 3.
2. Maimonides, "Hilchot Teshuvah" [Laws of Repentance], chap. 8, law 1; Babylonian Talmud, Kiddushin 39b.
3. Maimonides, "Hilchot Teshuvah" [Laws of Repentance], chap. 8, law 7.
4. Rabbi Moshe Chaim Luzzatto, *The Way of God* (New York: Feldheim, 1988), 1:3:11.
5. Babylonian Talmud, Sanhedrin 90a.
6. Babylonian Talmud, Ethics of the Fathers 4:21. Also see Luzzatto, *The Way of God*, 2:2:7.
7. *The Way of the Righteous*, trans. Seymour J. Cohen (New York: Feldheim, 1974), chap. 13.
8. Maimonides, "Hilchot Teshuvah" [Laws of Repentance], chap. 3, law 2. See the commentary of the Lechem Mishna.
9. Babylonian Talmud, Ethics of the Fathers 4:22. Also see Rabbi Eliyahu Dessler, *Strive for Truth* (New York: Feldheim, 1978), 31.
10. Maimonides, "Hilchot Teshuvah" [Laws of Repentance], chap. 8, law 2.
11. Deut. 14:1; Babylonian Talmud, Ethics of the Fathers 3:18; Rabbi Nosson Scherman, *The Complete Artscroll Siddur* (New York: Mesorah, 1984), 89. "With abundant love you have loved us."
12. Maimonides, "Hilchot Tefillah" [Laws of Prayer], in Mishneh Torah, vol. 2, *Ahava* [Love], chap. 15, law 6. Also see Maimonides, "Hilchot Teshuvah" [Laws of Repentance], chap. 3, law 5, for a discussion about (a) continuing to observe mitzvot (commandments) even after sinning and (b) those who have made numerous serious mistakes in life still being rewarded for their good deeds.

13. Luzzatto, *The Way of God*, 2:2:4.
14. Ibid. 2:2:4. "In His kindness, God created Gehennom to benefit man . . . so afterward a person can receive the true reward according to the goodness of their deeds."
15. Babylonian Talmud, Kiddushin 39b.
16. Maimonides, "Hilchot Teshuvah" [Laws of Repentance], chap. 9, law 1.
17. Babylonian Talmud, Berachot 5a. Also see Maimonides, "Hilchot Taniot" [Laws of Fasting], in Mishneh Torah, vol. 3, *Zemanim* [Times], chap. 1, law 2.
18. Babylonian Talmud, Ethics of the Fathers 4:19. Why the righteous suffer is an ultimate question that no one can answer completely. The answer was even hidden from Moses himself. You can't look into someone else's life and know why things happened to that person; only that person can know.
19. Ibid. Rabbi Yaanai points out that only you can know the lesson that God is trying to teach you.
20. Maimonides, "Hilchot Teshuvah" [Laws of Repentance], chap. 2, law 3.
21. Maimonides, "Hilchot Teshuvah" [Laws of Repentance], chap. 3, law 3.
22. Luzzatto, *The Way of God*, 2:2:4. "In His kindness, God created Gehennom to benefit man . . . so afterward a person can receive the true reward according to the goodness of their deeds."
23. Babylonian Talmud, Rosh Hashanah 17a.
24. Rabbi Yosef Karo, Shulchan Aruch, vol. 1, *Orach Chaim* [Way of Life], chap. 132, law 5. Also see commentary of Baer Haitev.
25. Maimonides, "Hilchot Teshuvah" [Laws of Repentance], chap. 1, law 3. Also see Maimonides, "Hilchot Teshuvah" [Laws of Repentance], chap. 7, law 2.
26. Babylonian Talmud, Rosh Hashanah 17a.

27. Rabbi Chaim Binyamin Goldberg, *Mourning in Halacha* (New York: Mesorah, 1991), 351.

28. Ibid.

29. Isa. 42:6.

SECTION TWO

1. Goldberg, *Mourning in Halacha*, 379, footnote 35.

2. Babylonian Talmud, Ethics of the Fathers 2:5.

3. Babylonian Talmud, Sanhedrin 74a.

4. Ibid. See commentary of Rashi: "How do you know you are more precious to God?"

5. Babylonian Talmud, Ethics of the Fathers 2:5.

6. Irving M. Bunim, *Ethics from Sinai* (New York: Feldheim, 1964), commenting on Ethics of the Fathers 2:5. Bunim points out that one can never truly assess the challenges others face, and therefore one person cannot judge another.

7. Karo, Shulchan Aruch, Yoreh Deah 2. See commentary of Chazon Ish in which he speaks of those who are the most distant from Jewish observance. He attributes the following to the Chofetz Chaim: "It is upon us to bring our people to Torah and Mitzvot with the 'handcuffs of love.'"

8. Maimonides, "Hilchot Teshuvah" [Laws of Repentance], chap. 3, law 2.

9. Babylonian Talmud, Sanhedrin 7a, discusses the concept that the beginning of a person's judgment is Talmud Torah (the study of Torah).

10. Babylonian Talmud, Ethics of the Fathers 2:18.

11. Maimonides, "Hilchot Tefillah" [Laws of Prayer], chap. 15, law 6. "Even if we make mistakes . . . we should keep on doing mitzvot."

12. Babylonian Talmud, Ethics of the Fathers 5:26.

13. Prov. 24:16.

14. Babylonian Talmud, Maakot 9a, discusses the concept that ordinarily, justice demands lesser responsibility from someone who is ignorant of the law. Jewish law indeed includes this principle, but this is only when someone is ignorant because he or she cannot learn what is right and wrong. For in a case in which one deliberately ran from knowledge, the Talmud says, "He should have learned, but he didn't, and is called "practically an intentional transgressor." (Also see Babylonian Talmud, Maakot 9a.) Therefore, one who studies (a) gets credit for the mitzvah of learning, (b) has strength to grow and is more likely indeed to become a better person, and (c) at least knows what is right and wrong and can make an intelligent decision. One who avoids study has none of these benefits, is culpable for not making an effort, and is called practically an intentional transgressor.

15. Maimonides, "Hilchot Talmud Torah" [Laws of Torah Study], in Mishneh Torah, vol. 1, *Madda* [Knowledge], chap. 1, vol 3.

16. Luzzatto, *The Way of God*, 1:2:1. It was taught by Chazal (the undisputed consensus of our sages) that "man is created only to take pleasure in God and to benefit from the splendor of His presence." When a great rabbinic scholar says that a concept was "taught by Chazal" without identifying a particular source, the concept is understood to be a core principle held by a consensus of the sages.

17. Gen. 12:1.

18. Maimonides, "Hilchot Yesodei HaTorah" [Laws of the Fundamentals of Torah], in Mishneh Torah, vol. 1, *Madda* [Knowledge], chap. 1, laws 1–6. Also see Sefer HaChinuch no. 25.

19. Deut. 14:1.

20. Maimonides, "Hilchot Yesodei HaTorah" [Laws of the Fundamentals of Torah], chap. 1, laws 8–9; Babylonian Talmud, Brachot 32a.

21. Regarding the idea that everything, including time, was created

by God, see Maimonides, "Hilchot Yesodei HaTorah" [Laws of the Fundamentals of Torah], chap. 1, laws 1–2. Also see Rabbi Aryeh Kaplan, *The Handbook of Jewish Thought* (New York: Moznaim Publishers, 1992) 10, note 20.

22. Babylonian Talmud, Brachot 5a; Maimonides, "Hilchot Taniot" [Laws of Fasting], chap. 1, law 2.
23. Exod. 20:1–16.
24. Babylonian Talmud, Brachot 5a.
25. Babylonian Talmud, Chulin 28a.
26. Maimonides, "Introduction to Mishneh Torah," in Mishneh Torah, vol. 1, *Madda* [Knowledge].
27. Ibid.
28. Babylonian Talmud, Kiddushin 2a.
29. See Babylonian Talmud, Kiddushin, where it states that the daughters of Rabbi Yaanai felt the same way.
30. Maimonides, "Hilchot Yesodei HaTorah" [Laws of the Fundamentals of Torah], chap. 7, laws 1–4.
31. Maimonides, "Hilchot Yesodei HaTorah" [Laws of the Fundamentals of Torah], chap. 10, laws 1–2.
32. Maimonides, "Hilchot Yesodei HaTorah" [Laws of the Fundamentals of Torah], chap. 9, law 1.
33. In Jewish thought and practice, the posture for accepting grief is always erect, symbolic of strength in the face of crisis and respect for the deceased.
34. Babylonian Talmud, Brachot 54a.
35. Babylonian Talmud, Brachot 7b.
36. Traditionally, women are not obligated in the saying of Kaddish and customarily arrange for it to be said by someone else.
37. Gen. 2:7.
38. Maimonides, "Hilchot Deot" [Laws of Character Refinement], in Mishneh Torah, vol. 1, *Madda* [Knowledge], chap. 7, law 3.

39. Rabbi Zelig Pliskin, *Love Your Neighbor* (Jerusalem: Aish HaTorah Publications, 1977), 194.

40. People who are truly wicked are not protected by this injunction. How Judaism defines one who is truly wicked is beyond the scope of this work; however, the definition does not include the people you ordinarily meet in daily life. The truly wicked are truly out of the ordinary.

41. Babylonian Talmud, Arachin 15a.

42. Maimonides, "Hilchot Deot" [Laws of Character Refinement], chap. 7, law 4.

43. Pliskin, *Love Your Neighbor*, 418. Please note that these laws are complex, and I have presented them here only in the briefest form.

44. Babylonian Talmud, Baba Metziah 23b.

45. Karo, Shulchan Aruch, vol. 1, *Orach Chaim* [Way of Life], chap. 1, law 1.

46. Maimonides, "Hilchot Tefillah" [Laws of Prayer], chap. 1, laws 1–3.

47. Karo, Shulchan Aruch, vol. 1, *Orach Chaim* [Way of Life], chap. 101, law 4.

48. Babylonian Talmud, Brachot 32b. There, Rabbi Elazar comments on the supreme significance of prayer.

49. Kenneth L. Woodward, "Talking to God," *Newsweek*, January 6, 1992.

50. The deepest understanding of this concept was withheld even from Moses. See Exod. 33:19, commentary of Rashi. Also see Babylonian Talmud, Brachot 7a.

51. Luzzatto, *The Way of God*, 4:6:7.

52. Babylonian Talmud, Sanhedrin 21b.

53. Maimonides, "Hilchot Meila" [Laws of Temple Violations], in Mishneh Torah, vol. 8, *Avodah* [Divine Service], chap. 8, law 8.

54. Allegorical tale. Source unknown.

55. Maimonides, "Hilchot Teshuvah" [Laws of Repentance], chap. 2, law 2.

56. Maimonides, "Hilchot Teshuvah" [Laws of Repentance], chap. 2, law 1.

57. Maimonides, "Hilchot Teshuvah" [Laws of Repentance], chap. 10, law 6. Maimonides explains that love is based on knowledge. The greater the knowledge, the greater the love.

58. Babylonian Talmud, Brachot 7b.

59. Medrash, Bereshit Raba. See commentary of Rashi.

60. Babylonian Talmud, Sotah 5a.

61. Num. 12:3.

62. Maimonides, "Hilchot Yesodei HaTorah" [Laws of the Fundamentals of Torah], chap. 5, law 7, discussing the recitation of the Shema.

63. Babylonian Talmud, Ethics of the Fathers 4:1.

64. Ibid.

65. Ibid.

66. Ibid.

67. Babylonian Talmud, Shabbat 31a.

68. Babylonian Talmud, Ethics of the Fathers 4:1.

69. Ibid., 6:6.

70. Babylonian Talmud, Kiddushin 31b. See Rashi.

71. Karo, Shulchan Aruch, chap. 240, laws 2–4.

72. Babylonian Talmud, Kiddushin 31a.

73. In the case of a violent, abusive parent, the law is more complex, and rabbinic guidance must be sought.

74. Maimonides, "Hilchot Mamrim" [Laws of Rebellion], in Mishneh Torah, vol. 14, *Shoftim* [Judges] chap. 6, law 5.

75. Medrash.

76. Gen. 18:1.

77. Babylonian Talmud, Shabbat 127a.

78. Gen. 32:29.

79. Maimonides, "Hilchot Yesodei HaTorah" [Laws of the Fundamentals of Torah], chap. 1, law 6.

80. Babylonian Talmud, Kiddushin 30a.

SECTION THREE

1. These are basic guidelines for observing the Jewish stages of mourning. For a more comprehensive look, please see Rabbi Maurice Lamm, *The Jewish Way in Death and Mourning* (New York: Jonathan David, 1988), and Rabbi Chaim Binyamin Goldberg, *Mourning in Halacha* (New York: Artscroll/Mesorah, 1991).

2. Gen. 7:4.

3. If a person passes away on a yom tov (for example, the first day of Passover), the burial is usually on the first day of Chol Hamoed. The shiva begins after the entire holiday of Passover is complete.

4. Traditionally, before the burial, the outer garment (shirt, blouse) of the mourner is torn. The tear for the loss of a parent is over the heart (left side); for all others it is on the right. The tear is a few inches long and may never be repaired, just as the loss of a loved one is forever. This garment is worn throughout the shiva.

5. Karo, Shulchan Aruch, vol. 1, *Orach Chaim* [Way of Life] chap. 395, law 1. "The first portion of the seventh day is counted as a whole day."

6. Nachamu Ami 21:12.

7. Chazon LaMo'ed 20:2.

8. Lamm, *The Jewish Way in Death and Mourning*.

9. The more I interviewed people for this book, the more the traditional way of paying a shiva call made sense. Time and time again, people told me that those who would come to comfort them truly had no idea what to say, so they would often say the wrong thing. One person told me that she wished people had just come and said nothing. When I told her that in fact that is exactly what is done at a traditional shiva, she sighed heavily and said, "That is the way it should be."

10. This is also why we break a glass at the end of the wedding ceremony. Even at the time of our greatest joys, we remember the destruction of the Temple in Jerusalem and the spiritual exile in which the Jewish people currently finds itself.

11. The placing of a tombstone has its origins in the time of the Torah when Jacob set up a matzeiva, a stone, for his beloved wife, Rachel (Gen. 35:20). The Medrash refers to this as the beginning of the custom of placing gravestones by the dead (Bereshit Rabbah 82).

12. One should not visit a grave site until the stone is erected.

13. Engraved on the tombstone, in addition to the person's Hebrew name, the father's Hebrew name, and the Hebrew date of death, are the Hebrew letters tof, nun, tzadi, bait, hey, which stand for "Tiyeh nishmatoh tzarur betzaror haim"—"May the soul be bound up in the bond of life." (For a woman it would be "nishmatah.")

14. If any of these days coincide with Shabbat or yom tov, one delays the visit until the following day.

15. The Talmud says, "Why do we go to the cemetery? In order that [the deceased] should ask for mercy for us." Babylonian Talmud, Taanit 16a.

16. These customs of praying for the souls of the departed and giving charity in their names are recorded in Karo, Shulchan Aruch, vol. 1 *Orach Chaim* [Way of Life] 621:6. See the commentary of Beis Yosef, who cites the custom of pledging donations. Also see the commentary of Rama, who adds the custom of Yizkor. The earliest source of the Yizkor custom is Midrash Tanchuma, Haazinu, which cites the custom related to Yom Kippur. Ashkenazi Jewry's custom of reciting Yizkor on Passover, Shavuot, and Shemini Atzeret is of later origin.

17. When the commemoration is on Passover or Shavuot, a candle should be lit from an existing flame as we do not kindle a new flame once yom tov has begun.

18. A virtually universal custom has those whose parents are still living leave the synagogue during Yizkor.

SECTION FOUR

1. For example, Deut. 18:11.
2. Mitch Albom, *Tuesdays with Morrie* (New York: Broadway, 1997), 80.
3. See Midrash Agada 47 concerning Jacob.
4. Exod. 20:15, commentaries of Nachmanides and Abarbanel. Also see Babylonian Talmud, Shabbat 89a, commentary of Maharsha.
5. Deut. 18:11.
6. Babylonian Talmud, Berachot 55a.

THE ONE HOUR PURIM PRIMER
Shimon Apisdorf

This book has everything a family needs to understand, celebrate, and enjoy Purim. User-friendly. Packed with great ideas for adults and children. Also includes a complete Hebrew-English Megillah/Book of Esther with brief explanations and commentary.

THE SURVIVAL KIT FAMILY HAGGADAH
Shimon Apisdorf

The only Haggadah in the world featuring the Matzahbrei Family, a loveable family of matzah people that guides you and your family through a delightful, insightful, spiritual, and fun seder. Featuring the "talking Haggadah" and a revolutionary translation. Never again will you read a paragraph in the Haggadah and say, "Huh, what's that supposed to mean?" This Haggadah is the perfect companion to *Judaism in a Nutshell: Passover*.

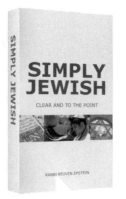

SIMPLY JEWISH
Rabbi Reuven Epstein

The ideal book to own and share with those seeking to gain a greater appreciation of the full tapestry of Jewish life. Simply Jewish is a concise, yet comprehensive book to virtually everything Jewish; the how to's and why's of Jewish life, holidays, practice, lifecycle events, and so much more. It's all here, beautifully illustrated and easy-to-read. (213 pages).

ROSH HASHANAH YOM KIPPUR SURVIVAL KIT
Shimon Apisdorf
Benjamin Franklin Award winner

There you are; it's the middle of High Holy Day services, and frankly you're confused. What you would like to do is stop the services, raise your hand and ask a few questions—but you can't. Enter, the *Rosh Hashanah Yom Kippur Survival Kit*. When you take this award-winning book to synagogue it's like having a knowledgeable guide sitting right next to you. Shimon Apisdorf, an internationally acclaimed author, masterfully blends wisdom, humor and down-to-earth spirituality in a book that is destined to become a classic—and has already become a close and trusted friend to thousands around the world.

"Thought-provoking, contemporary and coming straight from the heart. Apisdorf's guide will open the gates of prayer for a new generation."
—Rabbi Dr. Jonathan Sacks, Chief Rabbi Of England

BEYOND SURVIVAL: A Journey to the Heart of Rosh Hashanah, Its Prayers, and Life
Shimon Apisdorf

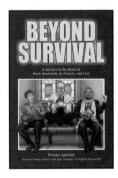

Beyond Survival is truly a guided journey—deep, unique, fun, and transformative. In the long awaited sequel to the classic *Rosh Hashanah Yom Kippur Survival Kit*, Shimon Apisdorf takes us to seemingly familiar places, and then opens our eyes to entirely new perspectives. Then he guides us to places we have never been before: to a world where Rosh Hashanah becomes the key to unlocking our hidden potential, where we discover the power of our soul, and where our prayers become pathways to remarkable growth.

Ideal Synagogue and Prayer Book Companion
It's known as the Silent Prayer, the Amidah, and the Shemoneh Esrei. Regardless of what you call it, *Beyond Survival* has got it. *Beyond Survival* includes the complete English and Hebrew Amidah (or whatever you call it), with spectacular insights and reflections that guide you to new vistas in prayer.

BLACK IS A COLOR
Stan Lebovic

As the son of a survivor of the Nazi concentration camps, Stan Lebovic grew up hearing the first-hand testimony of his father, to humanity's darkest moment. Nothing could beat back the horror of being tucked under the covers by an arm branded with death camp numbers.

When the life you are bequeathed does not resemble the life you are leading, there exists a great inner dilemma. Moreover, Stan Lebovic was raised, not only to believe in, but to embrace the very God responsible for the atrocities of his father's generation.

It is this struggle to have faith in the midst of madness, and the unique Jewish response to it, that is the subject of Black is a Color; a collection of works, rendered through art and prose, that express how traditional Jews found and still find, hope and faith in the midst of the deepest darkness.

It is an illumination of man's post-Holocaust spiritual stature; a search for the happy ending.

The artwork developed for Black is a Color, is meant to depict the heroic posture humanity has assumed in this post-Holocaust world, and present it to both man and God. For man it should serve as a reminder of the worth of his actions, and for God, a testament to the worth of His creations.

KOSHER FOR THE CLUELESS
BUT CURIOUS: A Fun, Fact-Filled, and
Spiritual Guide to all Things Kosher
Shimon Apisdorf

Kosher foods, kosher cooking, and the kosher dietary laws make up one of the most widely known yet least understood areas of Judaism and Jewish life. *Kosher for the Clueless but Curious* is the first book to ever present all aspects of kosher—including the kitchen sink—to readers who are filled with curiosity but are hungry for easy-to-understand information.

Includes a stunning 24-page full-color cookbook featuring recipes from two world-class chefs—Susie Fishbein, author of the best-selling *Kosher by Design* cookbook series, and Scott Sunshine, a veteran chef of the gourmet cooking industry.

INSPIRING DAYS

A collection of writings from a wide range of gifted educators, spiritual mentors, and writers. Reveals the great depth within Rosh Hashanah, Yom Kippur, Sukkot, and more.

INSPIRING LIGHTS

Another collection of remarkable essays that make the spiritual and intellectual lights of Chanukah shine brighter than ever.

All Books Available from The Afikim Foundation
212-791-7450 / www.afikimfoundation.org

About the Authors

LORI PALATNIK and RABBI YAAKOV PALATNIK are Jewish educators and writers. They have appeared on radio and television and regularly lecture throughout the world, illuminating classical Jewish wisdom for the contemporary mind and soul. Together they have been instrumental in the development of one of the most dynamic communities in North America—The Village Shul Synagogue and Aish HaTorah Learning Center in Toronto, Canada. They are currently the directors of Aish HaTorah in the Washington D.C. area (www.aishdc.com). Lori is the author of several other books that are available at www.amazon.com.

The Palatniks regularly counsel individuals and families who are dealing with the loss of loved ones, and are available for public speaking on a wide variety of topics. Contact them at LPalatnik@aish.com.

The authors encourage people seeking guidance in dealing with the loss of a loved one, or those desiring to deepen their Jewish knowledge, to contact the Aish HaTorah office in their area (www.aish.com), or to call the Association for Jewish Outreach Programs (AJOP) at 410-653-AJOP to locate the Jewish adult education organization in their area.